Triumphal Chariot of Antimony

Basil Valentine

with Annotations of Theodore Kirkringus (1678)

First published 2013
Copyright © 2013 Aziloth Books

British Library Cataloguing in Publication Data

A catalogue record for this book is available from the British Library

ISBN-13: 978-1-908388-96-4

Printed and bound in Great Britain by Lightning Source UK Ltd., 6 Precedent Drive, Rooksley, Milton Keynes MK13 8PR.

Cover Illustration: Sixth woodcut from the series in *Azoth*
by Basil Valentine (c. 1659)

TRIUMPHANT CHARIOT OF ANTIMONY

Since, Basil Valentine, by Religious Vows am bound according to the Order of St. Benedict, and that requires another manner of Spirit of Holiness, then the common State of Mortals exercised in the prophane business of this World; I thought it my duty before all things, in the beginning of this little Book, to declare what is necessary to be known to the pious Spagyrist, inflamed with an ardent desire of this Art; as, what he ought to do, and whereunto to direct his aim, that he may lay such Foundations of the whole matter, as may be stable; lest his Building shaken with Winds, happen to fail, and the whole Edifice to be involved in shameful Ruine, which otherwise, being founded on more firm and solid Principles, might have continued for a long series of time. Which Admonition I judged was, is, and always will be a necessary part of my Religious Office; especially, since we must all die, and no one of us, which now are, whether high or low, shall long be seen among the number of Men. For it concerns me to commend these Meditations of Mortality and Posterity, leaving them behind me, not only that honour may be given to the Divine Majesty, but also that Men may obey him sincerely in all things.

In this Meditation I found that there were five principal Heads, chiefly to be considered by the wise and prudent Spectators of our Wisdom and Art. This first of which is, Invocation of GOD. the second, Contemplation of Nature. The third, True Preparation. The fourth, The Way of Using. The fifth, Utility and Fruit. For he, who regards not these, shall never obtain place among true Chymists, or fill up the number of perfect Spagyrists. Therefore touching these five Heads we shall here following treat, and so far declare them, as that the general Work may be brought to light and perfected by an intent and studious Operation.

1. [GOD TO BE FIRST INVOKED]
Invocation of GOD must be made with a certain Heavenly Intention, drawn from the bottom of a pure and sincere Heart, and Conscience, free from all Ambition, Hypocrisy, and all other Vices, which have any affinity with these, as Arrogance, Boldness, Pride, Luxury, Mundane Petulancy, Oppression of the Poor, and other dependent evils, all which are to be eradicated out of the Heart; that when a Man desires to prostrate himself before the Throne of Grace, for obtaining bodily health, he may do that with a Conscience free from all unprofitable Weeds, that his Body may be transmuted into an Holy Temple of GOD, and be purged from every uncleaness. For GOD will not be mocked (which I earnestly admonish) as Worldly Men, pleasing and flattering themselves with their own Wisdom, think: GOD, I say, will not be mocked, but the Creator of all things will

be invoked with reverential fear, and acknowledged with due Obedience. And for this there is great Reason. For what hath Man, that he must not own to be recieved from this his Omnipotent Creator, whether you have respect to the Body, or to the Soul, which operates the Body? Hath no he, for sustention of this, out of his meer Mercy communicated to us his Eternal WORD, and also promised Eternal Salvation? Hath not he also provided food and cloathing for the Body, and all those things without which the Body cannot subsist? All these, by humble Prayer a Man obtains of that most excellent Father, who created Heaven and Earth, together with things Visible and Invisible, as the Firmament, Elements, Vegetables, and Animals. Which is so very true, that I am certainly assured, no Impious Man shall ever be partaker of true Medicine, much less of the Eternal Heavenly Bread. Therefore place your whole Intention and Trust in GOD, call upon him and pray, that he may impart his blessing to you: let this be the beginning of your work, that by the same you may obtain your desired end, and at length effect what you intended.

For the Fear of the Lord is the Beginning of Wisdom.

Whosoever purposeth in himself to seek after that, which is the greatest of Terrene things, especially the knowledge of every good thing, that is in the Creatures, and GOD hath liberally imparted to Men, and implanted (as to their effective power) in Stones, Herbs, Roots, Seeds, Animals, Plants, Minerals, Metals, yea and indeed in all things; let him cast away all Earthly thoughts, reject all that depends on them, and hope for freeness of Heart, and pray unto GOD with great lowlyness of mind: So doing, his hope of freeness may at length be turned into freedom. Which no Man will doubt, who knows, that he alone is GOD, who delivered Israel from all his Enemies; which deliverance he did in very deed effect, not only for Israel, but also for all Men making humble supplications to him, and praying with brokenness of Heart. Therefore let Prayer by the first point of our Admonition, which also is, and by us is called Invokation of GOD, which if made, not with Hypocrisy and a feigned Heart, but with such Faith and Trust, as that, with which the Centurion in Capernaum prayed; with such lowlines of mind, and confession of Sins, as the Woman of Canaan was endued with; with such Charity as the Samaritan shewed to the Man wounded in the way to Jericho, pouring Wine and Oyl into his wounds, paying his Charges in the Inn, and giving order he should be very carefully looked to; Lastly, if a Man's Christian Charity extends itself so far, as if he obtain what he prays for, he would willingly communicate of the same to his Neighbour, then he shall unobtainably obtain Riches and Health, the of his Prayer.*

*What the Author hath premised here at large, and elsewhere often inserted touching Piety, the worship of GOD, and Invocation of his Name, I purpose

neither to praise nor dispraise; Let them by judged by signs of his own earnest Piety, Arguments of his sincerity and signate Impresses of his fervent zeal (by so many Tautologies and Reiterations) often boiling up. Every Man, according to the Opinion of his mind, and the presuasion, in which he was educated from his Childhood, will more or less esteem of this. It was my business to translate the Authors writings into Latin, in such a Method and Order, as I thought would in no wise give any distaste to the delicate Palat of the Reader; also to indicate that, which seems pertinent to the business of every Chymist and true Spagyrist, and not to neglect the other. For since Piety is available for all things, as divine Oracles teach, and the principal exercise of Piety is Prayer; by which Celestial Gifts are obtained of GOD the giver of all good things; our Author wills, that unto him the mind by lifted up, even in the midstof the Operations of Chymistry full of labour and toil. If prayer effected no other thing, it certainly collects the mind (called away from all other things) into it self and renders it apt for that which is in hand; whence it comes to pass, that it reflects upon many things, and considers them, which otherwise would not enter the mind, if it set about its Work perfunctorily, and distracted with vaious Conceptions: And so by the help of Prayer we receive many things, which we (if not ungrateful) must needs acknowledge we have obtained from GOD. How often this is found to be of use in Spagyric Works every Man knows, that hath any time entirely devoted himself to this business; viz. how often those things which he long sought and could not find, have been imparted to him in a moment, and as it were infused from above, or dictated by soem good Genius. That also is of use in dissolving all Riddles, or Enigmatical Writings: For if you burn with a great desire of knowing them, that is Prayer; and when you incline your mind to this or that, variously discussing and meditating many things, this is Cooperation; that your Prayer may not be idle, or tempting GOD: yet this your endeavour is in vain, until you find the Solution. Nevertheless if you despair not, but instantly persist in desir, and cease not from labour, at length in a moment the Solution will fall in; this is Revelation, which you cannot receive unless you pray with great desire and labour, using your utmost endeavour; and yet you cannot perceive, how from all those things (of which you thought) which were not the Solution of the Enigma, the Solution it self arose. This unfolding of the Riddle opens to you the mystery of all great things, and shews how available Prayer is for the obtainment of things Spiritual and Eternal, as well as Corporal and perishing goods: and when Prayer is made with a Heart not feigned, but sincere; you will see that there is nothing more fit for the acquiring of what you desire. Let these suffice to be spoken of Prayer, which Basilius and all Philosophers with him do not vainly require, as an Introduction to Chymistry. For Piety is profitable for all Works, especially for Great Undertakings.

2. Next in order after Prayer is Contemplation, by which I understand an accurate attention to the business it self, under which fall these considerations first to be noted. As, what are the Circumstances of any thing, what the Matter, what the Form, whence its operations proceed, whence it is infused and implanted, how generated by the Stars, conformed by the Elements, produced and perfected by the three Principles. Also how the body of every thing may be dissolved, that is, resolved into the first Matter, or first Essence (of which I have already made mention in other of my writings) viz. how the last Matter may be changed into the first, and the first into the last.*

What are here set down, touching the true Theory of Philosophy, are compendiums of those things, which Philosophers have in os many Books (writ about the same business) revealed, shall I say, or concealed. Attend to the words of the Author, and you will see, that he perfectly knew that Spirit penetrating all things, which presides or bears rule in all things, yet is involved and absconded matter and defilements on every side; from which if once freed, it returns to the purity of its own substance, in which it produceth all things, and is all in all. To comment upon this, would be a work no less than the producing of all Books of Philosophers, compiled with such accurate study, and contending with so great contention about the Theory.

This Contemplation, which absolves the second part of our Admonition, is Celestial, and to be understood with Spiritual Reason; for the circumstances and depth of every thing cannot be perceived any other way, then by the Spiritual Cogitation of Man: and this Contemplation is twofold. One is called possible, the other impossible. The later consists of copious cogitations, which never proceed to effects, nor exhibit any form of a matter, which falls under the Touch. As if any one should endeavour to comprehend the Eternity of the Most High, which is vain and impossible, yea a Sin against the Holy Spirit, so arrogantly to pry itno the Divinity itself, which is Immense, Infinite, and Eternal; and to subject the incomprehensive Counsel of the Secrets of GOD, to humane Inquisition. The other part of Contemplation, which is possible, is called the Theory. This contemplates that, which is perceived by Touch and Sight, and hath a formed Nature in time: this considers, how that nature may be helped and perfected by Resolution of it self; how every body may give forth from it self, the good or evil, Venome or Medicine latent in it; how Destruction and Confraction are to be handled, whereby under a just Title, without Sophistical deceits, the pure may be severed and seperated from the impure. This Seperation is instituted and made by divers manual operations, and various ways; Some of which are vulgarly known by experience, others remote from vulgar experience. These are, Calcination, Sublimation, Reverberation, Circulation, Putrefaction, Digestion, Distillation, Cohobation, Fixation, and the like of these; all degrees of which are found in operating, learned, perceived and manifest by the same. Whence clearly appears what is moveable, what is fixed, what is white, red, black, blew, or green, viz. when the operation is rightly Instituted by the Artificer, for possibly the Operator may err, and turn aside from the right way; but that Nature should err, when rightly handled, is not possible. Therefore if you shall err, so that Nature cannot be altogether free, and released from the Body, in which it is help Captive, return again into your way, learn the Theory more perfectly, and enquire more accurately in the method of operating, that you may find the foundation and certainty in Seperation of all things. Which is a matter of great concern. And this is the second foundation of Philosophy, which follows the Prayer: for in that the sum of the matter lies, and is contained in these words. Seek first the Kingdom of GOD, and his Justice by Prayer, and all other things, which Man seeks in these Temporals, and he hath need of, either for the sustentation or health of his body, shall be added to you.

3. Next to the Theory, which researcheth out the inmost properties of things, follows Preparation, which is performed by Operations of the hands, that some real work may be produced. From Preparation ariseth Knowledge, viz. Such, as opens all the fundamentals of Medicine. Operation of the Hands requires a diligent application of it self, but the praise of Science consists in experience, but the difference of these Anatomy distinquisheth, *Operation shews how all things may be brought to light, and exposed to sight visibly: but knowledge shews the practice; and that, whence the true Practitioner is, and is no other then confirmation: because the operation of the hands manifests something that is good, and draws the latent and hidden nature outwards, and brings it to light for good. For, as in Spirituals, the way of the Lord is to be prepared; so also in these things, the way is to be opened and prepared; so also in these things, the way is to be opened and prepared, that no errour be from the right path, and the Process may be made, without devious errours, in the direct way to health.

*Manual Operation is chiefly required in this third Part, without which, every Operation, like a Ship wanting Ballast, floats and is uncertain. It is difficult to express this with a Pen; for more is learned by once seeing the work done, then can be taught by the writing of many Pages; yet if it be no offence to you, to peruse these Commentaries together with Basilius (in this so necessary part) will not a little help.

4. After Preparation, and especially after separation of the good from the evil, we are to proceed to the *Use of the weight or dose, that neither more, nor less then is fit, may be given. For above all things, the Physician ought well to know, whether his Medicament will be weak or strong, also whether it will do good, or hurt, unless he resolve to fatten the church yard, and with the loss of his fame, and hazard of his own soul.

8

By Use, the Authour understands what others call Dose; for what will a good Medicine profit you, if you know not in what quantity to administer it; that the same may rather heal, then hurt or kill. By experience only to learn this, is a work full of perilous casuality, yet the Discipline or knowledge of Doses was found out this way first, and afterward easily taught by Words. Where a living Voice is wanting, it is safer to be too timerous, then in any wise bold or adventurous, although of Antimony I can affirm, that being duly prepared it is as harmless a medicine as Cassia or Manna. The whole caution is chiefly about its use, after the first preparations; because it may still retain much of its own crude Venom.

5. After the Medicament is taken into the body, and hath diffused it self through all the Members, that it may search out those defects against which it was administered, the Utility comes to be considered; for it is possible that a Medicament diligently prepared, and exhibited in due weight, may do more hurt then good in some Diseases, and eem to be Venom rather then Medicine. Hence an accurate reflexion is to be made to those things, which profit or help; and they are diligently to be noted, that we may be mindful to observe the same in other cases.

Yet both in the *Use and Utility, this one thing is necessary to be considered, viz. whether the Disease be an external and open wound, or only an internal and latent evil: for as the difference of these is great, so the way of curation is not the same. Therefore the bottom of every Disease is to be knwon, that it may be understood, whether the same may be cured by external remedies only, or must from within be driven outwards.

That Indication is to be taken from things helping and hurting, is known even to Tyro's. But what the Author subjoyns touching internal and external curation, are not so rude, as not to deserve good Attention: And also those things which he permixeth with his own Satyrical Reprehension, if the Reader be so wise as to believe that Basilius intermixed them to deter the unworthy deriders of Chymistry from approaching to his sacred Arcanums, he will be wise for himself. For whilst others rail and swell with indignation, he gathers the fruit of the Authors Axioms, which as another Agent he scattered among these Thorns. Whilst you, O lover of Chymistry, peruse these, so long will I keep silence.

For if the Center of the Disease be within, such a Medicine must be given, as can search out, apprehend and restore that Center; otherwise the Physicians labour will be fruitless and in vain.

Moreover, if there be an internal Disease, which ariseth, and is fed from an internal Original, it must never be driven inward by external remedies; for great discommodity will thence ensue, and at length Death itself. Which may be understood by the similitude of a Tree; for if any one, whilst it germinates or flowers, repels the Humours to the Interiours, whence they proceeded to the nutriment of the earth; that Tree will be so far from bringing forth the desired Fruit by the flower, that a suffocation of the same ariseth from the violent conjunction of humours not finding any out-let. Therefore there is great difference between fresh wounds inflicted by Prick, Cut, or any other way, and the old which derive their Original from within. For the fresh wounds may be perfectly cured by external remedies only; but in those, which are nourished from within, an external application of Oyls, Balsoms, Unguents, and Plaisters profits little, unless the Internal Fountain be stopped, whence the humours flow to the external parts. When the Fountain shall be stopped, the Flux will cease, and the evil may easily be cured with Diet only. It is no great point of Art to heal any fresh wound; for this every Country-man can easily effect with crude Lard: but to remove all Symptomes which happen in wounds, and to dry up the Fountain of the evil, this is the work, and this the labour of the Artist.

[DOCTORS REPREHENDED]

Now come hither, you physicians, how many so ever there be of you, that arrogate to your selves the Title of Doctor of either Medicine, viz. of internal and external Diseases; understand ye the Title of your honour, and consult your own Conscience, and see, whether you recieved that from GOD, that is, possess it in verity, or whether you usurp it as a form, for honour sake. For, as much as Heaven is distant from the Earth, so vastly different is the Art of healing internal Diseases, from the Sanation of external wounds. If the Title be given to you by GOD, the same GOD will give a Blessing, Felicity, Health and happy events; but if your Title be vain, and only devised and assumed for ambition, all things will evilly succeed to you: your honour will fail, and you will prepare for your self Hell-fire, which can no more be extinguished, then it can be expressed by words. For Christ said to his Disciples; You call me Lord and Master, and ye do well, Therefore whosoever assumes a Title of Honour, let him see, whether he do well, and whether he ascribes not more to himself, than he knows and hath learned, which is the real abuse of this Title. For he, who will write himself Doctor of either Medicine, ought to understand, know, and be well skilled in both, viz. the Internal and External Medicine. Nor should he be ignorant of Anatomy, that he may be able to shew the Constitution of the Body, and discover from what Member every Disease proceeds, together with its Fountain and cause. Also remedies, with which he may cure the Disease, and circumstances of external Wounds, are to be understood by him. Good GOD! where will the Title be found, what will become of the Master, when an exact Trial shall be made, for discovering the ignorance of these Doctors of either Medicine?

In times past, long before my days, the Doctors of Medicine did themselves cure External wounds, and judged that a part of their Office; but in these times, they take Servants, whom they employ in these things, and this way the noblest of Arts is become a Mechanick Operation; and some of those who exercise it, are indeed so very rude, as they know not Letters, and scarcely know how (according to the Proverb) to drive an Ass out of the Corn. These, I say, profess, themselves Masters in curing wounds, and Doctors of Doctors; and to speak the truth as it is, they may by a better right glory in this Title, they thou magnificent Doctor, umbratical Chyrugion, and most ignorant Boaster of Titles, why do you style yourself Doctor of either medicine? What more now Master Doctor, what say you, most expert Chyrurgion? I pray be not offended at this, or take it amiss; for you your self will quickly confess, if you do but seriously consider wounds made by Prick or Cut, that you have as much knowledge in the cure of them, as is in the Brain of a dunghill Cock, which Children learning their A.B.C. are wont to set in the Frontispiece of their Primer.

[TRUE DOCTRINE, WHEREIN IT CONSISTS]

Therefore I persuade all Men, of what state or condition soever, who are desirous of Learning, from your Masters to search out the true Doctrine, which consists in Preparation, and afterward in the Use;

[OPERATIONS AND UTILITY GIVE EXPERIENCE] so they, or you, shall possess the Title assumed with honour, and Men will undoubtedly have confidence in you, and you will in very deed do them good, then will you to the Eternal Creator give thanks cordially without feigning. But let every Man seriously think with himself, what it is he ought to do, and what he is to omit, and whether he doth justly or unjustly use the Title assumed. For he, who assumes any Title, ought especially to understand the condition of that Title, and why he assumed it, or what the true foundation is. It is not sufficient, if anyone iwth the vulgar say (saving your reverence, let the more delicate Men pardon us, if we intending to speak to the purpose, make mention of putrefaction) this is egregious dung, it hath a strong and grievous ill savour, and know not how it comes to pass, that a Man, who perhaps eats food of a most grateful taste and odour, and well accommodated to his natural Appetite, thence makes excrement endued with qualities so contrary, and yielding an odour so very ungrateful, and repugnant to Nature: of which there is no other reason, then natural putrefaction and corruption. The same happens in all Aromatical well smelling things. It is the Philosophers part to enquire, what odour is, and whence it receives its virtues, and in what the virtue of it may be made manifest to true profit. For the Earth is nourished and fattened by stinking dung, and noble Fruit is produced of it. Of this matter there is not one cause only, but our Book would swell to an huge Volume, if we should but briefly hint at all natural Generations and mutations; yet Digestion and Putrefaction are the principal keys of them. For the Fire and Air make a certain Maturation, by which a Transmutation of the Earth and Water may follow; and this is also a certain mutation, by which of evil smelling Dung a most fragrant Balsam may be produced; and on the contrary, of most grateful Balsam ill favoured Dung. But perhaps you will say, why do I produce examples of so very rude and absurd? I do confess the example is taken from a Cottage, rather then a Royal Court; yet a prudent considerer of things, more accurately diving into the matter, will easily understand, what such examples intimate to him, viz. that of the highest things the lowest are made, and the lowest the highest, so that, of a Medicament is produced of Venome, and of Venome Medicine; of the sweet, bitter, acid, and corrosive; and on the contrary of the corrosive, another thing more profitable.

[NATURE ABSCONDED FROM MEN]

O good GOD, how much is Nature absconded from Men, so that she seems to disdain to be wholly seen by us? But since thou hast ordained so very short a time of our Life, and thou the Judge of all, reservest many things to thy self in the Creatures, which thou hast left to be admired, not known, by us, and of which thou alone wilt be the beholder and Judge, grant unto me, that unto my Life's end I may keep thee and my Saviour in my Heart, that besides health and necessaries of the body, which though hast liberally bestowed, I may also acquire the health of my Soul and Spiritual Riches; of which inestimable good I am freed from all doubt by that thy mercy, in which, for my soul, for me a miserable sinner, thou didst (on the Tree of the Cross) shed Sulphur and Balsom; which is indeed a mortiferous Venom to the Devil, but to us Sinners, a most present remedy. I do certainly heal my Brethren, as far as concerns the Soul, by Prayer, and in relation to the body, with apt Remedies; therefore I hope they will on their parts use their endeavour, that they with me, and I with them, may at length inhabit the Tabernacle of the Most High, and in him our GOD enjoy Eternity.

[SPIRIT VIVIFICATIVE, AND OPERATIVE]

But to return to my Philosophy of Antimony, I would have the Reader, before all other things, to understand, that all things contain in themselves operative and vivificative Spirits; which inhabiting in the Body feed and nourish themselves, and are sustained by the Body. Elements themselves want not these Spirits, which (the living GOD permitting that) whether they be good or evil, have their Habitation in tehm. Men and Animals have in them a living operating Spirit, which receding from them, nothing but a Carkass remains. In Herbs, and all things bearing Fruit, a Spirit of Sanity exists; otherwise they could not, by any Preparation, be reduced to Medicinal use. Metals and all Minerals, are endued and possessed with their own incomprehensible Spirit, in which, the power and virtue of all their possible effects, consists. For whatsoever is without Spirit, wants Life, and contains in itself no vivifying Virtue. Therefore, you are to know, that in Antimony also there is a Spirit, which effects whatsoever in it, or can proceed from it, in an invisible way and manner, no otherwise, than as in the Magnet is absconded a certain invisible power, as we shall more largely treat in its own place, where we speak of the Magnet.

[SPIRITS OF VARIOUS KINDS]

But there are various kinds of Spirits;* visible to the Intellect, and endued with Spiritual knowledge, which notwithstanding cannot (when they will) be touched or apprehended, as Natural Men are touched; [SPIRITS OF THE ELEMENTS] especially they, who have their fixed Residence in Elements, as are the Spirits of Fire, Lights and other Objects formally darting out Light from themselves: such are Airy Spirits, who inhabit the Air; Aqueous Spirits living in Waters; and Terrene Spirits living in the Earth, which we Men call Earthly Men, which are chiefly found in wealthy mines of the Earth, where they shew and discover themselves to us.

*What follow, seem somewhat confused, according to the Sentiments of certain Theologicians, who have held various opinions of Spirits residing in the Fire, Air, and other Elements; adjudging them to the Eternal Fire of Hell. All which with Basilius, we leave as unknown, to the Judgement of the Divine Knowledge. But what he himself subjoyns, touching the wonderful virtue and power of Antimonial and all other Chymical Spirits, which we our selves with so great admiration have often seen, we understand only of material Spirits; which certainly are endued with as great virtues, and effect things no less wonderful then those Spirits, which Phantastick persons (oppressed with Melancholy) affirm they see and talk with; yea I cannot remember that I ever found written or declared (by such, as taking a liberty of lying, endeavour to please or terrify others) any greater or more wonderful virtues then these Spirits have.

[SPIRITS WANTING SPEECH]

These Spirits are endued with Senses and Understanding, know Arts, and can change themselves into divers Forms, until the time of their Judgement; but whether a definitory sentence ought to be pronounced against them as yet, or no, that I leave to the Providence of the Divine Majesty, from whom nothing is hid. There are other Spirits, wanting speech, which cannot shew themselves visibly in the very act; and they are those which live in Animals, as in Men and the like, in Plants also and in Minerals; nevertheless they have in themselves an occult and operative Life, and manifest and discover themselves by their efficacious power of operating, which they contain in and bear about themselves, and most apparently give testimony of their virtue of healing, whensoever that (by help of the Art) is extracted from them, being accurately seperated from their body. After the same manner, the efficacious Spirit, and operative power of Antimony, manifests its gifts, and distributes them among Men, being first loosed from its own body, and freed from all its bonds, so, that it is able to penetrate, and render fit to be applyed to those Uses, which the Artificer proposed to himself in Preparation.

[ARTIST AND VULCAN OUGHT TO AGREE]

But the Artist and Vulcan ought to agree: [FIRE MAKES SEPERATION] the Fire gives seperation for an operative power, and the Artificer forms the matter. [EXAMPLE, OF A BLACKSMITH] As a Black-smith useth one sort of Fire, also Iron only is his matter, which he intends for forming divers Instruments. For some times of it he makes a Spit, at another time Horse-shoes, another time a Saw, and at length innumerable other things, every of which serves for that Use, unto which the Smith intended it, although the matter is but one, which he prepares for so many divers uses. So of Antimony various works may be made for different uses: in which the Artist is the Smith that forms; [VULCAN, THE KEY] Vulcan is as it were the key which opens; and Operations and Utility give experience, and knowledge of the Use. O! if foolish and vain Men had but Ears to hear, and true eyes with understanding, not only for hearing what I write, but for understanding the Arcanum and knowledge of the use; assuredly they would not suck in those insalubrious and turbid Potions, but hasten to these limped Fountains, and drink of the Well of Life.

[DOCTORS REPREHENDED]

Therefore let the World know, that I shallprove those pretended Doctors, who seem to be wise, to be mrere Fools and Idiots,and cause many unlearned Men (but such as are studious Disciples of my Doctrine) to become true Doctors in very deed. Wherefore I here solemnly cite and invite all Men, who earnestly aspire to knowledge, with a chearful mind, good Conscience, and certain hope, to embrace and become Spectators of our Doctrine, and accurately to peruse my Writings and Informations; for so, at length, they (being possesors of what they sought) will extol and commend me after death, rendering my mortal name immortal, with their perpetual remembrance of my praises, as long as the World endures. But if when I am dead, any one be pleased to institute a disputation in the Schools against me, my writings will fully answer all his Objections, and I am assured my Disciples will never forget the benefit received from me, by which they will obtain the Empire of Truth, which ever was to me, and always will be to them, sufficient to suppress a Lie to the Worlds end.

[ANTIMONY OF 2 KINDS]

Also let the well meaning and sincere observer of Art know, that there are two kinds of Antimony very different from each other: one is fair, pure, and of a golden property, and that contains very much Mercury, but the other which hath much Sulphur is not so friendly to gold as the first, and is distinguished by fair long and white shining streaks. Therefore one is more fit for Medicine and Alchemy, then the other: as when the Flesh of Fishes iscompared with the Flesh of other Animals, although both these are, and are called Flesh, yet each of these very much differs from the Flesh of the other; even so of Antimony the difference is the same. Many do indeed write of the Interior virtue of Antimony, but few of tehm ever taught the true Foundation of the virtues with which it is endued, or found out which way, or in what manner it recieves them; So that their Doctrine is founded upon words only, exists without any true foundation, and they themselves lose the fruit they hopes to receive by such Writings. For to write truly of Antimony is a work that requires profound Meditations, a mind largely unfolding itself, and knowledge of its manifold Preparation, and of the true Soul of it, in which all the Utility is cited, and which being known you may be able to give an indubitate Judgement, of what evil or good, Venom or Medicine is latent therein. It is not a matter of small moment by a true Examen to search into Antimony, and thereby to penetrate fundamentally into its Essence, and through earnest study to attain the final knowledge thereof, that the Venenosity of the same (against which unskilful Men ignorantly exclaim) may be taken away, and it be changed and prepared into a better State, becoming a Medicine fit for use and void of Venom.

[ARTISTS VEX, WREST AND TORMENT ANTIMONY]
Many Artists intending to Anatomize Antimony, have divers ways vexed, wrested and tormented the same, in such wise as it cannot be well described in Words, much less believed; yet, the matter being truely examined, they effected nothing. For they sought not its true Soul, and therefore could not find the feigned Soul of it, which themselves sought. By the black Colours a mist was cast before their Eyes, so that they could neither observe the true Soul itself, nor know it. [ANTIMONY COMPARED TO A CIRCLE] For Antimony like unto Mercury, may fitly be compared to a round Circle, of which there is no end; in which the more diligently any Man seeks, the more he finds, if Process be made by him in a right way and due order. Yet the Life of no one Man is sufficient for him to learn all the mysteries thereof. It is Venom and a most swift poison, also it is void of Venom and a most excellent Medicine; whether it be used outwardly or inwardly. Which is a thing hid form most Men by reason of their own blindness; and they judge it an incredible, foolish and vain work, because (through their ignorance) it is unknown to them, who can no otherwise be excused, then that they deserve the name of Stupidity: yet that is not to be suffered in them, because they desire not to learn or be better informed, either here, or elsewhere.

[ANTIMONY ENDUED WITH THE 4 FIRST QUALITIES]
Antimony is endued with all the four first qualities; it is cold and humid, and against it is hot and dry, and accommodates it self to the four Seasons of

the year, also it is volatile and fixed. The volatile part of it is not void of Venom, but the fixed is free from all venenosity; which is so very strange, as it may be reputed one of the seven Wonders of the World, of which so many Writers have discoursed, not knowing themselves what they writ. [ANTIMONYS VIRTUES INEXHAUSTIBLE] There hath been no *Man before me, and at this day there is none found, who hath so thoroughly learned the power, virtue, strength, operations, and efficacy of Antimony, or so profoundly penetrated into all the Energy thereof, as nothing more is latent in it unfound out, or which cannot be brought to light by experience. If such a Man could be found he would be worthy to be carried about in a Triumphal Chariot, as in times past was granted to Monarchs and potent Heroes, after they had happily fought Battles, and were returned with Victory. But I fear, that many of our Doctors will be constrained to provide a Chariot for themselves.

*Here the Author speaks largely in commendation of Antimony. Read, read (I say) O Lover of Chymistry, and you will find nothing Hyperbolical, nor anything Thrasnick. Basilius in speaking as he doth, hath not exhausted the Praises of Antimony; because no Man unto this day could ever experience all its Virtues. We have seen many of its Effects, and many new Effects are daily found by curious Searchers, yet many more remain unknown. So that, as in Fire is an inexhaustible Fountain; (for the more you take from it, the more it gives) so in Antimony is an inestimable Treasure of new Virtues. For if from it you extract its Acetum a thousand times, it will a thousand times, yield new Acetum. Nature seems to have made choice of this Mineral, therein to hide all her Treasures. Therefore not without reason hath Basilius made for it a Triumphant Chariot, which is daily enriched with Spoyls taken from the Camps of Ignorance.

For the Masters of this terrene World are so intangled with their own Thoughts, that they seek nothing from Antimony but Riches, and forget to search its utility for medicine, and the Health of the Body, which notwithstanding ought above all things to be sought, that (being brought to Light) the wonderful Works of our GOD may be made manifest, and the Glory given to him, with great thankfulness. It is not to be denied, but that more of Riches and Health may be found in it than either you all, or I myself, can believe: for I profess my self no other than a Disciple in the Knowledge of Antimony, although in it I have seen, experienced and learned more than you, and all such as you are (who arrogate to yourselves great skill therein) either have learned, or ever can learn. Yet no Man should therefore be troubled, or despair of Benefits; but because the World, indulging their own Ingratitude, have neither esteemed, nor with due Reverence acknowledged the Munificence of the Most High, but have preferred Riches before Health, GOD hath spread as it were a Spider's Webb before their Eyes, that being blind they might not know the Secrets of Nature absconded in the Form of this Mineral.

[RICHES REQUIRED BY ALL]

All men cry out Rich, Rich we would be. I confess you all aspire to Riches, and with the Epicure say, The Body must first be provided for, the Soul may at length also find somewhat; and with Midas (as in the Fable) you desire that all things whatsoever you touch may be turned into Gold. Hence it is, that so many seek their desired Riches in Anatomy: But because they accept not that Gift of the Creator with a grateful Heart, which before all Things should be procured, and cast the Love of their Neighbour behind their back, therefore they in vain look the Horse in the Mouth; for they know his Age and Strength no more than the Guests at the Marriage-Feast in Cana of Galilee knew the wonderful Work, which Christ there wrought, when he turned Water into Wine. They knew, that Wine was Water, and that the Water was turned into Wine, they perceived by the Taste; but how that Transmutation happened was hid from them. For the Lord JESUS, our Saviour, reserved the Supernatural Work to himself, as a Testimony of his Omnipotency. Wherefore I say, it is every Man's duty, to search out the Mysteries and Arcanums, which the Creator hath insited in all Creatures; for although (as we said) it is not Credible, that we Men can thoroughly learn and penetrate all Things; yet we are not forbid to inquire into them, since by Study and Diligence so much may be effected, as although through some defect a Man may be hindred in such wise, as he cannot attain to the desired Riches and perfect Sanity, yet he may acquire enough to occasion him not to repent of his Labour, but rather to minister unto him matter of Joy and Rejoycing, that he sees himself so far an Adeptist, as he stands always obliged to render thanks to his Creator.

[SOLUTION WHEN NECESSARY]

Therefore, whosoever desires to become a perfect Anatomist of Antimony, the first thing to be considered by him is Solution of the Body; and in order to this, he must take it in a convenient place, and propose to himself the right way, that he be not seduced into devious Paths. Secondly he must observe the Governance of the Frie, taking Care that it be neither too much, nor too little, or too hot, or too cold. For the summ of all is sited in an exact Governance of the Fire; by which the vivifying Spirits of Antimony are extracted, and loosed from their bonds, and so rendered capable to manifest their Effects operatively. Also he must take great Care, that this Operative Virtue be not mortifyed and persih Adustion. [DOSE, OBSERVABLE] Thirdly the Use or Dose is to be observed by him, that he may administer it in due manner, knowing the Measure, as I above mentioned, when I spake of the five principal Heads requisite in the Exercise and Practise of Chymistry; but here I only hint at it cursorily by way of a parable.

By Resolution the sum of the Matter is proposed, but by Fire it is prepared to profit. For a Butcher cuts out an Ox, and divides it into parts, but no Man can profitably enjoy this Flesh, unless he first boyl it by Fire, by which Operation the

Red substance of the Flesh is changed and prepared into white Aliment. If a Man constrained by hunger, should eat that Raw and Red flesh, it would be Venom to him rather than Medicine; because the natural Heat of the Stomach is too weak to concoct and digest that crude Body. Hence, my dear Friend, you may conclude, that since Antimony hath greater Venom, and a more gross Mineral Body than Animal Flesh (as by the above recited common Example I have already shewed) it will also prove more perillous, if used Crude, without remain Venom, which will suddenly kill the Sick.

[VINEGAR, NOT TRANSMUTABLE INTO WINE]

Therefore the Venenosity of Antimony is so to be taken away, as it may never against be converted into Venom, after the same manner, as Wine, which being once, by putrefaction and corruption turned into Vinegar, never afterward yields any Spirit of Wine, but always is and remains Vinegar. but on the Contrary, if the Spirit only of the Wine be seperated, and the Aquosity left by itself, and the same Spirit afterward exalted, it will never in any wise be changed into Vinegar, although it should be kept an hundred Years; but will always remain Spirit of Wine, no otherwise, then as Vinegar remains Vinegar.

[WINE, TRANSMUTABLE INTO VINEGAR, HOW]

This Transmutation of Wine into Vinegar is a wonderful Thing; because somewhat is produced from Wine, which was not before in its vegetable Essence. In which it is also to be noted, that in distillation of Wine the Spirit first comes forth; but (on the contrary) in distilling Vinegar the Phlegm first comes, afterward the Spirit, as I have shewed above in its own place, where I also made mention of this Example. [SPIRIT OF WINE, VOLATILZE] Therefore Spirit of Wine makes Bodies volatile, because itself is volatile; [SPIRIT OF VINEGAR, FIX] but Spirit of Vinegar fixeth all Medicaments, as well of Minerals as Vegetables, and renders them solid, so that they apprehend things fixed, and expel fixed Diseases.

[ANTIMONY CONTAINS ITS OWN VINEGAR]

Consider and observe these things diligently; for this principal Key is of great concern. Therefore Antimony, which contains in itself its own Vinegar, ought to be so prepared, as all its Venenosity may be taken away, and he, who useth it, conceives no Venom thereby, but rather drives away and casts out all Poison from himself, by the use thereof.

Believe not only Basilius, but me also, with the same Faith and sincerity affirming to you; this is the first Key, this is the principla part of the whole Art, this opens to you the first Gate, this will also unlock the last, which leads to the Palace of the King. But as I said, not only beleive, but also consider and observe.

Here you stand in the Entrance, if you miss the Door, all your Course will be Error, all your Hast Ruine, and all your Wisdom Foolishness. He who obtains this Key, and knows the Method (which is called Manual Operation) by which to use it, and has strength to turn the same, will acquire Riches, and an open Passage unto the Mysteries of Chymistry.

Therefore Preparation of Antimony consists in the Key of Alchimy, by which it is dissolved, opened, divided and seperated; as in Calcination, Reverberation, Sublimation, etc. as we declared above it. Also in extracting its Essence, and in vivifying its Mercury; which Mercury must afterward be precipitated into a fixed powder. Likewise by Arts and due Method, of it may be made an Oyl, which is effectual wholly to consume that new and unknown Disease, which the French, in their Warlike Expeditions, brought into our Regions. The same is visible in other Preparations, derived from the Spagyrick Arts and Alchimy; as for Example: [EXAMPLE, OF BEER] If anyone would make Beer of Barley, Wheat, or other Corn, all these degress must be most perfectly known to him, before he can from those Grains extract their most subtil Essence and virtue, and reduce the same into a most efficacious Drink. First, the Grains must be so long steeped in Water, as until they be able sufficiently, to open and resolve themselves (as I, when I was a Young Man, travelling into England and Holland, diligently observed to be done in those places) this is called Putrefaction and Corruption. This Key being used, the Water is drawn off from the Grain, and the macerated Corn is laid on Heaps close together, and left so for a due time, until it spontaneously conceive heat, and by the same heat, germinating, the Grains adhere each to other: this is Digestion. This being finished, the Grains which adhered in their Germination, are separated, and dryed, either in the Air, or by Heat of Fire, and so hardened. This is Reverberation, and Coagulation. [CALCINATION, VEGETABLE, WHAT] When the Corn is thus prepared, it is carried to the Mill, that it may be broak and ground small; this is Vegetable Calcination. Afterward, by heat of Fire cocting these Grains, the more noble Spirit of them is extracted, and the Water is imbibed with the same; which without the aforesaid Preparation could not have been. This way the crude Water is converted into Beer, and this Operation (though I speak but rudely) is and is called Distillation. [HOPS, THE VEGETABLE SALT OF BEER] The Hops, when added to the Beer, is the Vegetable Salt thereof, which conserves and preserves from all Contraries, endeavouring to corrupt the same. This way of boyling Water into Drink, by extraction of the Spirits from the Grains, the Spaniards and Italians know not, and in my native soil of Germany about the Rhine, few are found skilled in this Art.

After all these works are performed, a new Seperation is made by Clarification, viz. of the Drink, in this manner: a little Yeast or Ferment is added, which excites an internal motion and Heat in the Beer, so that it is elevated in it self, and (by the help of time) Separation of the dense from the rare, and of the pure from the impure is made; and by this means the Beer acquires a constant virtue in Operating, so that it penetrates and effects all those Ends, for which it was made and brought into use: which before could not have been; because the Spirit, the Operator was hindered, by its own Impurity, from effecting its proper Work.

In Wine also doth not Experience teach the same? That cannot, before the time come, in which the Impuritys may be separated from it, so very perfectly and efficaciously perform its own Work, as after Separation of the pure from the impure: which by Drunkeness is manifest; for Beer or Wine unsettled, and not purifyed, give not forth from themselves so much Spirit for inebriating, as after Clarification. But of this no more. After all the aforesaid, a new Operation may be instituted, by Vegetable sublimation, for separation of the spirit of the Wine or Beer, and for preparing it by Distillation into another Drink of Burning Wine, which may also be made of the Lees or Dregs of Wine and Beer. When this is done, the Operative Virtue is separated from its own Body, and the Spirit being extracted by Fire, forsakes its own unprofitable dead Habitation, in which it was commodiously hospited before. Now, if this Burning Wine, or Spirit of Wine, be rectifyed, an Exaltation is made by often distilling it, and by a certain method of Operating, the pure part (free from all Phlegm and Aquosity) may be so concentred, and as it were condensed, as one Measure of it may effect more, then twenty or more could have done before. For it sooner inebriates, and is swift, volatile and subtil for penetrating and operating.

*Here I admonish you, whosoever you are, who desire to be taught by my Writings, and hope to obtain Riches and a true Medicine from Antimony, that you would not carelessly peruse my Intention, in which is no letter writ in vain, and which hath not a certain singular signification for your Instruction.

*Come hither you Traveller, stay your Journey here. Contemn not or flighty pass over this tautological, but not impertinent, Admonition; often in your mind have recourse to this Description of Beer, search, contemplate, and weigh all Things, perhaps in this turbid and famous Gulf, you will find the Fish you look not for. If in this Light you yet be blind, I know not any Collyrium will profit you: if with so certain a manuduction you cannot pass on to the work itself, I know not who will lend you a Staff, or what Demonstration can direct the Journey of a Stupid Man. Believe, read, meditate, labour, and spare the use of so many Chymical Books, which distract you with the Error of various ways, this one tells you all things.

Yea, I here solemnly affirm, that there are many words dispersed here and there in my Writings, to which if the Reader give heed as he ought, and know in what Fundamentals the principal Heads of the matter are sited, and as it were buried, he will have no Cause to repent his often turning over the same Leaves, but will esteem every word as much, as a piece of Gold coin. For you know, that althought the Examples by me proposed, sound harsh, as delivered in a rude manner, yet they contain in them somewhat that is excellent and of great Moment. Yet I am not here ambitious to procure Authority or praise to my Writings, which is not my Business, nor would it become me: for when the Operation of them shall be brought to Light, they will acquire praise enough to themselves. [EXAMPLES OF BEER, WHY PRODUCED] I purposely and willingly produce Examples so rude and common, because the power of Antimony and the true Virtue thereof, deeply and profoundly absconded in its inmost parts, is to be searched out. I was willing, by these gross Examples to lead you by the hand, and shew you the way, that by them you might attain to the Thing itself, and not at the very first err from the Gate; for so doing you would long wander, and never bring your Operation to the desired End. [ANTIMONY COMPARED TO A BIRD IN THE AIR] For Antimony is like a Bird, which is carryed through the Air and as the Wind drives it, so it turns itself which way that wills: here, in this Case, Man acts the Part of the Air or Wind and can drive and move Antimony, at his pleasure, and repose it in such a place, as himself chooseth: he can imbibe it, with a yellow, red, white or black Colour, according as he desires it should be, and as he rules and governs the Fire; because in Antimony (as in Mercury) all Colours are found, which no Man should wonder at, considering how many Things Nature bears absconded in her Bosom, which neither you nor I are able to comprehend in many days.

[ANTIMONY COMPARED TO A BOOK] If a book happen to be given to a Man, that is unlearned, he knows not what is signified by that Writing, or what that Scripture intends; for it is hid from his Eyes, and he stands amazed, as a Cow at the sight of a new Door. But if unto that unlearned Man, anyone suggest the Explication of the Book, and teach him not only the matter contained therein, but also the use of the same, the Man no more admires it, as an Art; but by this means it becomes to him a Common Thing, the Reason and Operation of which he understands, and by his own Study can learn, conceive, and comprehend the Utility so perfectly, as now none of those Things, which were contained in the Book , are hid from him; because he hath learned both to read and understand what is written therein. Such a Book is Antimony to those, who know not of the Art of Reading; therefore I faithfully admonish all, who desire to be partakers of its Utilities, to bend their mind to know and pronounce the letters thereof, that so they may acquire the Art of Reading that Book; and in such a manner, that (as in a School) they may be removed from Form to Form, when he who hath rightly gained Experience, shall preside as Rector, and judge of that, which in Trial is most worthy: for One is worthy to be preferred before another, in the Possession of that.

[DOCTORS REPREHENDED] But here, what comes into my mind, and ought in no wise to be passed over in Silence, I think good to mention; viz: that at this Day many are found who exclaim, and rashly pronounce Crucifige, Crucifige, against all those, who prepare Venoms into Medicaments, by which (as they say) many Mortals perish, or, if they escape with Life, live miserably; such are Mercury, Arsenick, Antimony, etc. and this Clamour is chiefly made by those, who (if it please the GODS) are called Doctors* of Medicine, yet indeed understand not what the difference is, between Venom, and Medicine, but are wholly ignorant how Venom may be prepared, so as to pass into a salutary Medicament; and instead of its malignity, put on a better Nature.

*Basilius somewhat indulgeth his own Genius, inveighing against False-Phyisicians, whose ignorance (in his time) was so very greate, as they contemned every sublime Preparation of Medicine, which he himself, and Chymists with him did profess; proscribing the same as unprofitable, perillous, and hurtful: against whome, it is not strange, if the Chymists (on the other hand) rose up with some small vehemency, and endeavour courageously, by assistance of their Knowledge, and Conscience, to break through that rout of unskilful Men; but the best Things are not allways the most prosperous. Chymists overcame by the Justice of their Cause, but were overcome by Number: yet, having verity and goodness on their side, thy fought with so great Confidence, as they were certainly assured they should bear away the Victory; which our Author here shews, and Paracelsus (prophesying of the Coming of Elias the Artist) did presage would be. And certainly unto me (seriously considering how greatly chymists have in these times improved their Knowledge) the Dawning of that Day hath opened itself, since I behold so many Rays of the approaching Sun.

[VENOM PREPARED RESISTS POISON] Against these I do in a special manner exclaim and protest, against these, I say, who (ignorance of Preparation) exhibit Poison to Men: for Mercury, Auripigment, Antimony, and such like, are venoms in their Substance, and unless rightly prepared remain Venoms. Yet after a Legitimate Preparation, all their Venenosity is broke, extinguished and expelled, so that no part of them remains, but what is Medicine, which resists all internal Venoms, although most deeply rooted, and radically destroys the same. For Venom, being in such a manner prepared, as it can no longer hurt, resists all Poison, which is not as yet prepared, and so very well prepares and subjugates it, as it is compelled with the same to put off its own venomous Nature.

[DOCTORS REPREHENDED]
Here I shall raise a great Contention among the Learned; for I know they will doubt what these my Words should signify, as whether what I affirm and write be possible to be done or no; and they will be divided into several Opinions there-about. Some will judge it is in no wise possible, that from those Things, of which we treat, the venenosity should be wholly taken away; nor do I wonder, that

they persist in that Opinion, since the Doctrine of like Preparations is absolutely unknown to them, who have not the least thought of that, which leads to the Knowledge of thse more profound Mysteries. Yet a small part of these Men will with me be constrained to acknowledge, it is possible a vile Thing may be changed into a Better. For you (you Doctors I mean) must confess to me, that your purpose is to reduce that Evil, from which the Disease had its Original, into a better State. Go to then; will you not also grant, that if any Evil be in those Things, of which Medicine is to be made, the same Evil must be converted into a better State, that it may so much the better perform its operation, and more powerfully and profitably act, without any notable peril? But since unto very few as yet is known, or by Experience found, the Way, by which a Man ought to proceed in these Preparations, a very small part of these will assume and contend for the Opinion I here affirm, and publicly profess: for very many will be carried away with the greater Rout, crying, Venom, Venom! which Voices, whilst I hear them, put me in mind of those wild Clamours, by which the Jews required the Saviour and Redeemer of the World, that he might suffer the Punishment of the Cross, often crying out Crucify him, Crucify him, whom they proclaimed to be the highest, most present, most pernitious, and cursed Venom, when as indeed he was the noblest, supreme, most glorious and most profitable Medicine of our Souls, which was to deliver us from the Death of Sinners, from the Devil, Hell⊓ and all Misfortunes. Although those proud Pharisees and Lawyers neither could nor would understand this, nevertheless he both then was, and will be to the end of the World, and after it to all Eternity, the same superexcellent Medicine: and neither the Devil, nor Death, nor the very Gates of Hell, nor any Creature, how powerful, or perverse soever, can effect anything at all, whereby to overthrow this Truth.

[KINGS, AND PRINCES, MISINFORMED BY DOCTORS]

So I hope, yea doubt not (although all vagabond and circumforaneous Medicasters, all Physicians resident in Cities, and how many soever there be, that profess themselves Masters of any part of Medicine, do all together contrive what they can, and exclaim against Antimony) but that the same Antimony will triumph over the ingratitudes of all those unskilful Men (for true Physicians and such as are always ready to learn, I touch not here) and by its own power and virtue acquired after due preparation, will overcome and tread under foot all its Enemies. But, on the contrary, those ignorant false Judges, and pertinacious contemners of Antimony, because they know not the Truth, together with the proud and blood-thirsty Jews, shall perish, and be cast into the Abyss of Hell. How ridiculous those magnificent, and to themselves only wise Doctors, seem to me, who deterr Emperors, Kings, Princes and all other Great Men, and seriously admonish them not so much as to touch such Medicines with their Lips, because they are noxious, venomous, and every way perillous, I will not here declare, since

I see them only to judge according to their own Opinion, without entertaining any Observations of other things, the Knowledge of which they have not before acquired by their own Contemplation, and therefore cannot judge of any thing else, or otherwise than they have learned. Therefore to these I say, if there be any Man, that hath taken so strong a Poison, as present Death is necessarily expected to follow, I will (provided the Man be left wholly to my Care) give him an Antidote by me prepared which shall continually resist that Venom, and quickly expel it out of the Body. But I little care, whether you Mr. Doctor, who do neither know this Thing, nor ever would apply your mind to know it, do slight the same, and repute it as a ridiculous, and altogether false tale; it is sufficient for me, that I am able (but if praise worthy, let praise be given to GOD) to prove and defend the Truth thereof. For I myself have experienced it, I have made, I have prepared, I have prescribed this Medicine, and there wants not a sufficient number of Witnesses to confirm it under Hand and Seal.

[DOCTORS REPREHENDED]

And whensoever I shall have occasion to contend in the School with such a Doctor, who knows not how himself to prepare his own Medicines, but commits that Business to another, I am sure I shall obtain the Palm from him: for indeed that good Man knows not what Medicines he prescribes to the Sick; whether the Colour of them be white, black, grey or blue, he cannot tell; nor doth this wretched man know, he only knows, that he found it so written in his Books, and thence pretends Possession (or as it were Possession) by Prescription of a very long time: yet he desires no further Information. Here again let it be lawful to exclaim, good GOD, to what a state is the matter brought! what goodness of mind is in these men! what care do they take of the Sick! Wo, wo to them! in the day of Judgement they will find the fruit of their ignorance and rashness; they they will see him whom they pierced, when they neglected their Neighbour, sough after Money and nothing else; whereas were tehy cordial in their Profession, they would spend Nights and Days in Labour, that they might become more learned in their Art, whence more certain health would accrew to the Sick Labour is tedious to them, they commit the matter to Chance, and being secure of their Honour and content with their Fame, they (like Brawlers) defend themselves with a certain Garrulity, without any respect had to Conscience or Truth; Coals seem wonderful strange, and as out-landish Wares to them, therefore they spare the Money, that should be bestowed in them, as if they intended to lay it out to a better use. Vulcan himself, viz. the Prepairer of Medicaments, is not found among them; for their Fornaces stand in the Apothecaries Shop, to which tehy seldom or never come. A Paper Scrol in which their usual Recipe is written, serves their purpose to the full, which Bill being by some Apothecaries Boy or Servant recieved, he with great noise thumps out of his Mortar every Medicine, and all the Health of the Sick.

24

My GOD, change, change these times, and put an end to this arrogant Pride, overturn those Trees, lest they swell up to Heaven, throw down those Giants lest tehy accumulate all Mountains; and defend those, who seriously managing their Business, faithfully serve thee, that they may be able to stand against these their Persecutors. I seriously admonish all those in our Monastery, bound by the same Vows with me, that they would with my self Night and Day pray unto GOD, that he would so illuminate these Enemies of true Medicine, as tehy may execrate their own Error, and acknowledge the Glory of GOD, and his Power insited in the Creatures, and perceive the Clearness latent in them, by Preparation and Anatomy (as it were speaking in their Ears) which otherwise surrounded and covered over with external Impurities, would deeply be concealed, and never brought to Light. But I trust the Creator of all Things, (both of those which fall under our Sense, and of those that are remote from our Senses) will benignly hear our Prayers; that, if not whilst I and my Brethren live, yet after our Death, such a Conversion of Things and Men (GOD answer these desires) may follow, as that thick and obscure Veil may be taken away from the Eyes of our Enemies, and they by true and infallible Illumination, obtain a clear sight, that tehy may find their lost Groat: which GOD, the eternal Governour of Time and Things of his Grace and Mercy grant.

But it is fit, that I, who intended to publish a certain Discourse of Antimony, in all its Numbers Absolute, should begin with the *Name itself.

*Poets do often posit in the midst of their Poems, Histories or Fables of Princes, that by a continued Series of Things, they may the more easily attain their End, which is to delight their Readers: Chymists for another end use the same Medium. For since their purpose is to teach the Readers so, as they may only be understood by those, who wholly devote themselves with a fervent desire to the Study of that Science, they keep not that Order, which proceeds from the beginning to the End by Mediums. Therefore our Author, at length coming to treat of the name of Antimony, whence it took beginning, acts as anohter Man addicted to some Scholastic Order: but by and by turning from this Discourse, he answers an Objection, before it is made by Interrogation; viz. whether from Antimony all its Venom may be taken away, the possibility of which he proves by very profitable and significant Examples.

The Arabians, to whom in times past this Mineral was known, did in their Language call it Astinat; but the Chaldeans called it Stibium; among the Latines at this day the name of Antimony is used, by which name they first of all signified it. We Germans in our Language have given it a Name, which seems to express a certain property of its Nature, for since it is seen to consist of a certain streiked

Matter, and of it may easily be made Glass endued with various Colours, which proceed therefrom, we have called it Spies-glass, as if we should say streiked Glass. From which Variety of the Name, by a prudent Judgment a singular Collection may be made, viz. that Antimony was knwon, and greatly esteemed, and its virtue and Utility observed and brought into use by the Arabians, Chaldeans, Latins, and our Germans: but afterward, the Heresies of various Opinions arising, the use was vitiated, and its Virtue and Glory first obscured, and afterward wholly extinguished. Of which there is no Reason to Doubt; for nothing is more probable, than that Truth should suffer Dammage and Shipwrack by the Oppression of Enemies. For who knows not the Malice of the Devil, which by Reason of our Sins and Blindness is very often permitted by GOD. The Devil is the perpetual Enemy of Mankind, who imploys all his Strength, and all his Deceits, and omits nothing, which in himself is, to prevent the Knowledge of the profit of true Medicine, and to exterminate its use; knowing well enough, that by that means the power and glory of GOD is obscured, and those Sacrifices of the praises of men are impeded, by which they gave thanks to GOD, because he hath insited as it were the Rays of his Goodness in the Creatures, whence they may obtain Health by a natural auxiliary.

But since to discourse of the name of Antimony, is not to our purpose, we will desist from this Matter. For all the Praise of Antimony consists in the Preparation thereof, which is made for perfecting the Virtues infused in it from Nature by the Author of Nature. Therefore my discourse shall be of this, handling it and its known Virtue, and I will endeavour to make my Name immortal. Yet before I come to declare the Virtue of Antimony, since I above confessed, that it is meer Venom, I would have you know and diligently note, that Venom is able to draw Venom to itself, because like itself, much sooner and much more than any other Thing of another Nature.

[VIRTUE OF UNICORNS-HORN PROVED]

Now let any Reader consider, and observe it as a Thing worthy of Note, that the true Unicorns-horn, sophisticated by no fallacy, repels all Venom from itself, nor can it assume or draw to itself anything of Venom, as is manifest by Experience. Let a living Spider be put in a Circle made of Unicorns-horn, and out of this Circle it cannot go, or pass over the Unicorns-horn, for it shuns whatsoever is adverse to Venom. But if the Circle be made of venemous Matter, it is not to be doubted, but that the Spider will go out of it, and pass over that Venom like it self. Note this Experiment, make a piece of Silver hollow, and put it in Water, that it may float like a Boat, and put Venom into it, then hold a piece of true Unicorns-Horn, as nigh to it as you can, but so as you may not touch it, that Unicorns-Horn by its spiritual Virtue will drive the Silver from it, so that it will flie away like a Duck, which swimming on the Water flies, when it perceives the Snares of the Fowler ready to entangle it. But on the contrary, Nature in a wonderful manner loves and follows its own like, as appears by this Example. Put a piece of pure and fine Bread in a dish full of Water, so as the Bread may swim upon the Water, hold a piece of true Unicorns-Horn close to it, yet so as it touch it not; and if you leisurely move the Unicorns-Horn the little piece of Bread will follow it. Nature so much loves its own like, and so much hates what is unlike itself, as this flies and that follows. Therefore let our Doctors consider, that Venom by a certain Magnetick Power Attracts Venom, and those things which are void of Venom, do in like manner draw to themselves things pure, and wanting a Venomous quality.

[VENOM TAKEN AWAY TWO WAYS]

Therefore Venom may be taken away two ways; first, by its Contrary, which resists Venom, as already is related of the Unicorns-Horn. Secondly,by Like, when Venom by a certain Magnetick power draws Venom to itself. But the Venom which must heal Venom like itself, ought first to be so prepared, as its Venom may pass into Medicine, and by its own attractive virtue, assume the other to and expel it with itself. [EXAMPLE OF SOAP] Of which thing you have a most clear Example of Soap: That is compounded of Oil and other fat ingredient Matters, which seem to be, and in very deed are, more apt to foul, than cleanse Linen; but because in the Boiling of Soap, especially by the help of Salt, a certain Separation and Preparation is made, the Soap is rendered most apt to draw to itself and wash out all foulness and filths from Linen and other things: so indeed may Venom in a certain manner, by Antecedent Preparation be accommodated so, as to be no more Venom, but a Medicament, it draws to itself all other Poison, casts it out, and restores the man to his pristine Purity and Health. Now since our Discourse hath led us so far, and we have begun to open Nature so much; that the truly Studious of Medicine (though hitherto ignorant of this) may clearly know, what Good or Evil is latent in Nature, what is Venom and what is harmless; which is a thing hath not as yet been found out by Doctors, by reason of their own supine negligence; and that the Truth thereof may be demonstrated and also confirmed, it will not be amiss to produce certain Experimental Examples, which may discover the Truth, and refute the false Opinions of others. [EXAMPLE OF AN EGG] Put an Egg, which in the Winter is congealed with Cold, into very cold Water, there let it lie for a due space of time, and the Ice will externally adhere to the Egg-shell, but the Cold be extracted from the Egg itself, and restored to its pristine vigour and intireness. [EXAMPLE OF A MEMBER BENUMMED] Again, if any Member be benummed with Cold, let not the Patient neglect himself, but apply cold Snowwater round about, so one Cold attracts the other, and the Member is restored. [EXAMPLE OF A MEMBER INFLAMED] On the contrary, if any one have a Member inflamed, let him apply to that Inflammation an hot Matter; as for example, Spirit of Wine, which is mere Fire, or the Quintessence of Sulphur, and he will in very deed find, that Heat is attracted by Heat, in a certain Magnetick manner, and like to rejoice in like, and not only to asswage the pain and heat of the inflamed Member, but absolutely to restore the same to its pristine strength.   [EXAMPLE OF FROGSPAWN] Yet lest this our purpose should not be fully enough confirmed by Examples, I will also add another, by way of Supplement. Take Frog-Spawn in the Month of March, and laying it on a Board dry it in the Sun, when dry reduce it to Powder, and strew of this Powder, upon wounds made by Venomous Vipers or Serpents; by this means such Wounds will be so prepared, as they may be perfectly healed by other Medicaments applied thereunto. Or otherwise, if Linen cloths be often moistened in Frog-Spawn, and as often dried, and that Linen cut into small pieces and applied to Wounds, they effect the same, as the aforesaid Powder would have done. [EXAMPLE OF A TOAD] But that the very foundation of this Truth may more clearly be declared; take a venemous Toad, dry him in the Sun, shut him up in an Earth closed Pot, and by burning reduce him to Ashes; then having taken out the Ashes, and reduced the same to Powder apply of that Powder to a Wound made by Venom, and this Poison attracts the other Poison, and joins it with itself. Why so, I pray? Because by this Burning, which is the Calcination of the Toad, its interior Virtue is made manifest, and efficacious for operating; so, that Like can attract like, and especially Venom, to itself. Therefore firmly perswade yourself, that this Truth is infallible and immuatable, which I have here proposed to you and others by Example. If anyone afflicted with the Pest, do diligently observe this, he will find the Truth of those things I have here above mentioned: the Astrum of Sol, from which (as from an operative and all vivifying Sun) all things in their kinds universally arise; therefore I determine that in the potency of Gold, more than in all other Things, is an Operating Nature; that is, in its own Astrum, whence both itself, and all Metals and Minerals, in the Beginning, received their first Nativity and Propagation of Generation. Touching which more may be said, when I shall manifest to you the Astrum of Sol, and commend the same most religiously to your Conscience.

[ANTIMONY, ITS ASTRUM]
    After the same manner process is to be made with Antimony, which hath the same Operations with corporal Gold; yet of the Astrum thereof I now speak not. [ANTIMONY SPEAKS OF ITSELF] For I know (saith Antimony) it behoves me, before that, to fear and tremble; although in many principal Arcanums of Medicine, I far excel it; yet universally I am able to effect none of those Things, which the Astrum of Sol (confirmed by the Testimony of Celestial Verity) is able to produce. The Astrum of Mercury I omit, because I my self have my descent from the same Original with it: but as to a Celestial penetrating power of Operating, I give the first place of Dominion to the Astrum of Sol.

[VULCAN, A MASTER IN HIS OWN ELEMENTS]
    My Writings and Books, composed by Experience, properly follow and answer each to other; as one metal (as to its virtue) is observed and esteemed by

another, and must by Fire be proved of what value it is. So these my Sayings, or Writings, or Medicaments, ought to be brought into the Schools, as tending to one Scope and End. Into the Schools, I say, where Riches obtain to themselves (as it were) an Hereditary place, and instead of that take away all the Honour, which is due to Vulcan only, who can boast himself to be a Master in his own Element of Fire. Which may be shewed by Example, and a true and manifest Proof. [EXAMPLE OF STEEL AND A FLINT] When most hard Steel is struck with an hard and solid Flint, Fire excites Fire by vehement Commotion, and accension, drawing forth the occult Sulphur, or the occult Fire is manifested by that vehement Commotion, and enkindled by the Air so, as it truly and efficaciously burns; but the Salt remains in the Ashes, and the Mercury thence takes its flight together with the burning Sulphur.*

You, who read this most simple Comparison of Steel and a Flint, slack the Reins of your Admiration, and seriously ask yourself, whether there can be found out anyway or Method, by which from this Stone and Cold Iron may be extracted, a Substance, of which one only Grain (but why do I speak of a Grain?) of which the hundred part of a Grain can in a very short time Convert a great Mass of some rude Matter, into the most splendid and most pretious of all Things; yea, into fire most profitable for Mankind? This is possible, and is dayly done, when the fixed is made Volatile, and the Volatile again fixed. He that hath understanding, let him understand, and cease to defame the admirable virtues of Chymical Works.

[MEDICINE, INEFFECTUAL IF NOT SEPARATED FROM ITS IMPURITY]
So here also understand, that Antimony ought in a certain Method so to be handled, as its Mercury may be separated from the Sulphur thereof, in a Natural Manner. Now as Fire, which lies absconded in Matter, unless it be made manifest, and can be demonstrated, is profitable for nothing, is not (as I may say) tangible by the Hands, nor can it effect any thing to purpose; so Medicine can effect nothing that is excellent, unless it be first separated from its Grossness, rectified and so discharged of Impurities, clarified and brought to Light by due Preparation, as is manifest in all Things: for when Separation of the pure from the impure is made, and all that is mountanour or terrestrial is segregated from the pure Metal, then the desired Harvest is to be expected. Hence it is manifest, that Fire can effect nothing, before it is in a certain manner opened and set at Liberty, that before it is in a certain manner opened and set at Liberty, that it may operate. Therefore, to comprehend much in few Words, I say, this is the Condition of Antimony. Whatsoever is occult and absconded from the Knowledge of the Vulgar, that injoys the Name and Honour of Art, viz. as long as it lies hid; but so soon as it is discovered and made manifest, Art hath end, and it becomes a Mechanick Work; as I have than once declared in other of my Books.

[EXAMPLE OF BEES]

A Bee sucks Honey from Flowers, with such Art as the Almighty hath insited in it, in which Honey is latent a Virtue, Juice, and Corroborative Power, of which a Medicine is made, as is obvious to the Eyes of all Men. [EXAMPLE OF A CORROSIVE VENOM OF HONEY] Now, from that Honey, of a sweet and most pleasant Taste, a violent Corrosive and present Venom may be prepared; which perhaps no man, unless he who hath learned it, will believe; no man certainly considers this, unless he be a diligent Observer. Yet for this Cause Honey is not to be condemned, nor is it to be said, that although it hath a most grateful Sweetness, yet it is a Corrupt Medicine; because a Corrosive may be made of it: but it should rather be said, that Corruption proceeds from the Physicians ignorance, who knew not how duely to prepare it. Here I am willing to teach the ignorant Physician, to free him from the last Judgement. [HONEY, HOW PREPARED] For Honey is prepared of the Superfluities of Brute Animals, by which the Grounds and Fields are fattened; in those Grounds arise Flowers, Herbs, Fruit-trees of various kinds, from which the Bees suck a most noble Quintessence: by this is made the Alteration and Generation of one Thing into another, viz. into Aliment of another Form and Taste, which in no wise agrees with the former, and that is called Honey. Of such Honey is prepared a Food most grateful, pleasant and fit for man, and for many Things most profitable. Of the same may be prepared a Poison most hurtful to Man and Beast.

[NATURE TO BE FOLLOWED]

Therefore, do you Searcher of Nature, of what Age, Sex, Fortune, or Condition soever, follow me and Nature. I will shew you the Truth, without any Mixture of falsity, drawn from the very Foundation. I will make you understand, who proceeds rightly, and who unadvisedly. I will teach you to separate the Good from the Evil, the Highest from the Lowest. For of Antimony, if its Venom be first changed into Remedy, is made a Medicine, which eradicates, and like Fire penetrates, prepares and by cocting consumes all Diseases. [QUINTESSENCE OF ANTIMONY, WHAT] Wherefore Antimony is first to be prepared into a true Stone, which is the Quintessence thereof; and because, in its Operation it is altogether like unto Fire, (when reduced to its Coagulation) it shallby me be named the Stone of Fire. when this Stone of Fire is rightly prepared, as in the End of this Treatise I will further show, its Medicinal Virtue consumes all noxious Humours, purifies the blood in the highest Degree, and performs all that may be effected by Aurum Potabile.

[DOCTORS REPREHENDED]

Therefore, I pray you, my unexperienced Doctor, who have neither learned my Preparation, nor conceived the Use, not to judge from a false suspicion, and your own ignorant Thoughts; but set about the Work itself, and learn how the

Preparation of Antimony ought to be made, how you should further proceed with it, how its Venom is expelled and separated, and Salutary Medicine posited in the place of it, and exalted. When I say* you shall have performed This, then at length will you be able to judge of the difference, and understand those things, which before were very far remote from your Knowledge.

*Here again the Author waxeth hot against false Physicians; but do you read on, and after this Heat he will give you a profitable Doctrine, which you may soon find in Aqua Fortis and Spirit of Wine.

[DOCTORS REPREHENDED]

O you wretched and to be pitied Medicasters, who painted with a Fucus, breath out I know not what Thrasonick Brags, and pass over Mountains wanting Foundation, walking through Clouds in your own Thoughts, and know not where at length you shall rest your Foot: you, I say, I admonish to consider what you will answer, in the Extreme Judgement of the Son of GOD. Seek, and when you have found, convert what you find to use, and so performing your Office commit the Rest to GOD, who will give success, and never leave you destitute of help. But you infamous men, more mad than Bacchanalian Fools, who will neither learn, nor foul your Hands with Coals, judge not lest you procure Judgement to be pronounced against you, which your Childrens Children may write down to your shame in an undeleble Character.

Every Physician ought above all Things to take Care, that he do neither less nor more, than procure the Restitution of Health lost, not instituting his Curation contrary to Nature, or deviating from her direct Intention. [EXAMPLE OF SPIRIT OF WINE AND AQUA FORTIS] When Spirit of Wine is poured upon Aqua Fortis a vehement Ebullition is made, and these two Natures will not easily permit themselves to be together; but he, that knows how by Distillation to conjoin them and unite them, according to the true Intention of the Philosophers, he may use them in many things for good. [EXAMPLE OF OIL OF TARTAR AND VINEGAR] After the same maner, Oil or Liquor of Tartar, and Vinegar made of Rich Wine, act each upon other, for they hate and fly from each other, as Fire and Water, although they proceeded from one and the same Matter. Therefore the Physician ought in a special manner to be mindful, to understand all Circumstances from the Sick very exactly, and consider the same being understood that in Curing he may use such Means, as are fit to remove the Disease, lest the Patient be injured by the Medicine. As for Example, when Iron is dissolved in Aqua Fortis, if you suddenly pour Oil of Tartar upon that Solution, you shall difficultly preserve Glass from breaking; for the contrary Natures, like unto Gunpowder, take Fire, and break the Glass. Of all these Things, our Gown Doctors know nothing at all; therefore they have no other Defence for their Ignorance, than Silence only.

[DOCTORS AND APOTHECARIES REPREHENDED]

You titular Doctors, you I speak to, who write long Scroles of Receipts: you Apothecaries, who with your Decoctions fill Pots, no less than Those (in Prince Courst) in which Meat is boiled for the sustentation of some hundreds of men: you, I say, who hitherto have been blind, suffer a Collyrium to be poured into your Eyes, and permit them to be anointed with Balsom, that the most thick skin of Blindness may fall from your Sight, and you behold the Truth, as in a most clear Glass. [AUTHORS PRAYER] GOD grant you Grace, that you may know his wonderful Works, and the Love of your Neighbour be rooted in you, that you may search out true Medicine, which the Ruler of the Heavens hath, by his own omnipotent hand, and his ineffable and eternal Wisdom, from above infused in, impressed on, and communicated to his Noble Creatures, for the Good of Mankind; whence man may find help in his greatest Necessity, and Counsel for Health in his Diseases. Why do you, miserable Worm of the Earth, and food of Worms, look so intently on the Rind or Shell, and neglect the Kernel, being unmindful of your Creator, who formed you according to his Image; when as you ought to give thanks to him, and with diligent Study to search out his Works, exceeding Nature herself? Return and look into your self, there behold the Image of your own ingratitude, that you may be ashamed of yourself, especially because you have not search out those things, which the most wise GOD, for the good of Mortals; hath infused in his Creatures; by knowing which, you might have offered unto him the most acceptable Sacrifice of Praise and Gratitude.

But I will put an end to this Discourse, lest my Tears (which I can scarcely keep in, from continually falling from mine Eyes) should blot this my Writing, and whilst I deplore the Blindness of the World, I blemish this Lamentation, which I would have known to all men. I am a man Religious, incorporated in a most holy Order, in which I will persevere, as long as it shall please the Omnipotent GOD, to animate this miserable Body with Vital Spirit: therefore I must not write other things, or otherwise, than is agreeable to this State. But had I the Office of a Secular Judge, I would lift up my Voice, and sound a Trumpet in their Ears, that those deaf men may hear, who hitherto would not acknowledge the Truth, but out of Ignorance, without Cause, falsely and slanderously persecute, calumniate, condemn, disparage, and meditate how they may totally suppress the same.

But thou, O Lord GOD, who dwellest in the Highest, who art called and truly art the GOD of Rest, who sitting in the Supreme Throne of Majesty, governest Heaven and Earth, which thou hast created, who conservest the Stars, and ordainest the Course of the Firmament in its Motion according to thy Command, before whom all Creatures tremble, which are found in the Earth, or in Heaven, and the Infernal Spirits are astonished with unexpressable dread, be pleased, I pray to look down upon the Transactions of this most ungrateful World, and teach them inwardly to know those Things, which thou hast outwardly and visibly proposed to the Sons of Men, that thou mayest be praised in thy Throne, known in thy Verity, and adored in thy immense Majesty. As for myself, I am unworthy and miserable man, give thanks unto thee, for thy great and infinite Gifts and Benefits of Riches and health bestowed on me, and laud thy Majesty for ever for the same. More, O my Father and Lord, I neither can, nor am able to desire in this perishing World.

[ANTIMONY, ITS ORIGINAL AND ROOT]

Now, that we may write of Antimony, and begin our Discourse from the very Foundation, whence Antimony acquires its Empire, Triumph and Glory, by which it is exalted to perfect Operation, we must before all Things discover the certain Original of its Root: how it is generated in the Earth, to the Dominion of what Stars it is subjected, and what Elements have throughly digested it, and which tehy be, that have brought it to Maturity. Antimony is no other than a Fume, or (as I may otherwise call it) a Mineral Vapour, which is genited from above by the Stars, and afterward by the Elements deduced and digested to formal Coagulation and Maturity. Here it is to be noted, that Antimony hath acquired its Essence, Virtue, Power, Operation and Quality, from the same Principle, Root and Essence, whence Vulgar Mercury is produced; yet with more firm Coagulation, so that it is brought to an harder Essence, than the living or running Mercury of the Vulgar hath. The Reason of this is, because it hath assumed from the three Principles, a little more of the Substance of Salt, than Common Mercury. For although of all the three Principles, it hath the least part of Salt, yet it hath assumed more of the Essence of Salt, than common Mercury, whence unto it hath happened such a Coagulation. Hardness in everything is from Salt, which vulgar Mercury hath not. For it hath a very small part of Salt, but in it, in a spiritual manner, is insited a certain more hot Spirit of Sulphur; therefore it always flows, and cannot be brought to Coagulation, unless by the help of other Metallick Spirits, which endued with a very great Virtues, are chiefly found in the Matrix of Saturn, without which it cannot be fixed, unless by him, who possesseth the Stone of Philosophers, by which its three Principles may be brought to a concordant Equality, and then it acquires such a Body, as will melt, flow, and abide the Hammer, like all other Metals: other wise Mercuy is and will be fluid Mercury, until its volatility be this way taken away. [MERCURY, NOT FIXED BY ANIMALS AND VEGETABLES] Hence it is known, that all Animals and all Vegetables are too weak to fix Mercury into a malleable Substance (as many have in vain endeavoured) because all these have not a Metallick Nature. [MERCURY, WITHIN AND WITHOUT MERE FIRE] Mercury, within and without, is no other than meer Fire; therefore it is not combustible by any Fire, no Fire can apprehend it so, as to alter its Essence, but it suddenly flies and resolves itself into a incombustible Oil Spiritually; [MERCURY UNVARIABLE AFTER FIXATION] or after its fixation it remains so invariable, as no strength or power of men is sufficient again to alter it. And whatsoever can now be made of Gold may then also be made of it by Art; because after Coagulation it is altogether like Gold: for it with Gold hath one and the same Root, Stock, or Production originally.

But since I purpose not in this place to discourse more largely of Mercury, and intend only simply (yet truly) to describe the very Foundation of Antimony, from true and certain Principles, I will cease to speak of Mercury, and proceed to a further Declaration of Antimony. Yet, whatsoever I have proposed by way of Similitude touching Mercury*, for an Introduction and further Consideration, is not written in vain, or to no purpose; but to the end, that the very Beginning of Antimony may be more clearly understood, which (as I before shewed) received its original, as it were Mercurially, with it.

*Which so miserably perplexeth all the Students of this Art: what our Mercury is, which is the Matter of the Stone, which is found every where and in all Things, is here briefly and clearly manifested. Therefore our Author Basilius doth not in Vain invite your Attention. All the Light I am able to add to this Clearness, would rather obscure, than illustrate the same: therefore, with him, I admonish you to attend.

[MATTER, OF ALL METALS AND MINERALS, ONE]
Wherefore most diligently think on this; often bear in mind, observe and understand, that all Minerals and Metals together, in the same Time, and after the same manner, and of one and the same principal Matter, are produced and genited. That Matter is no other, than a meer Vapour, which is extracted from the Elementary Earth by the Superior Stars, as by a Sidereal Distillation of the Macrocosm: which Sidereal hot infusion, with any Airy-Sulphureous Property descending upon Inferiors, so acts and operates, as in those Metals and Minerals is implanted spiritually and invisibly a certain Power and Virtue, which Fume afterward resolves itself in the Earth, into a certain Water, from which Mineral Water all Metals are thenceforth generated and ripened to their Perfection; and thence proceeds this or that Metal or Mineral, according as one of the three Principles acquires Dominion, and tehy have much or little of Sulphur and Salt, or an unequal Mixture of the weight of them, whence some Metals are fixed; that is, some constant and stable, some volatile and easily mutable, as is seen in Gold, Silver, Copper, Iron, Tin and Lead. Besides these Metals, other Minerals also are generated of the three Principles, according to the Communication and Participation of the unequal weight of them: as are Vitriol, Antimony, and many other Marchasites, or other Electrums, and Minerals, which for brevity sake we here omit.

But Gold, in its Astrum and Beginning was imbibed with a much more perfect Sulphur, and a much more perfect Mercury, than all other Metals and Minerals, and therefore its operative Virtue is much more potent and more efficacious, that the Astrums of other Metals: Yea, all Virtues whatsoever are dispersed in other Metals, and many more than them, are found in the Astrum of Gold only. Moreover I say, when that one thing is brought to further Maturity by Fire, it contains more Perfection, than all Metals and Minerals together. There is one only Mineral, of which I have often made mention already, in which is found a Sulphur of Sol, equally as strong and powerful, yea more potent and more strong, than in Gold itself: so also, there are two kinds of Metals found, in which this Predominancy powerfully Triumphs, of which at this time I have neither will nor disposition to write; but I am willing to keep within the Bounds I have set myself in treating of the Essence of Antimony, touching which I purpose now to speak.

[ANTIMONY, ITS THREE FUNDAMENTAL PRINCIPLES]

Therefore Antimony is a Mineral made of the Vapour of the Earth changed into Water, which Spiritual Sidereal Transmutation is the true Astrum of Antimony; which Water, by the Stars first, afterward by the Element of Fire, which resides in the Element of Air, is extracted from the Elementary Earth, and by Coagulation formally changed into a tangible Essence, in which tangible Essence, (viz. whence Antimony is formally made) is found very much of Sulphur predominant, of Mercury not so much, and of Salt the least of all three; yet it assumes so much Salt, as it thence acquires an hard and immalleable Mass. [ANTIMONY, ITS PRINCIPLE QUALITIES]/The principal Quality of it is dry and hot, or rather burning, of Cold and Humidity it hath very little in it, as there is in Common Mercury; in Corporal Gold also is more Heat than Cold. These may suffice to be spoken of the Matter, and three Fundamental Principles of Antimony, how by the Archeus in the Element of Earth it is brought to perfection.

Yet the Lovers of Chymistry should not think this Philosophick Reason by me alleged of absolute necessity to them, nor need they be solicitous to know, in what center the Astrum of Antimony rests, or from what root it flows; but should rather desire to learn the Utility and use thereof; viz. which way it ought to be prepared and reduced to its State, that tehy may know its Virtue, Power, and Operation, touching which in times past so many Things have been written, and to this Day are mentioned, and spoken of by all men of all States and Conditions. For the Learned, as well as the Unlearned hope to have their ardent and insatiable Desire satisfied by This; therefore I will not detain the Reader with ambiguous Discourses, or tedious Delays, but simply teach every Thing, which I by great Study and Diligence (which I have often imployed about Antimony) could find out touching the Essence of Antimony. For no man, by reason of the shortness of Life, can know or search out all its Arcanum's: because in Preparation of Antimony, one new Wonder follows another perpetually; one Degree succeeds a former Degree, Colour follows Colour, and one Virtue, Power or Operation always manifests it self greater than another.

And, to begin here I say, Antimony is meer Venom, not of the kind of the least

Venoms, but such, as by which you may destroy Men and Beasts, so venomous a power is diffused through the whole Substance of this Mineral. Hence ariseth the common Exclamation of all men. [KINGS, AND PRINCES, MISINFORMED BY DOCTORS] For the People, unskilful Doctors, and all Those, to whom the ground of true Medicine is unknown, do with one mouth proclaim it Venom, Venom! Poison, say they (as I myself above confessed) lies in Antimony. For this Cause let us dissuade all men from its use; for it endangers the Health and Life. Therefore Doctors resident in Princes Courts, admonish Monarchs, Princes, and other Potentates not to use Antimony. Other Scholasticks cry out, Beware, you in no wise admit Antimony into Medicinal Use; for it's meer Poison: these the Inhabitants of Cities and Villages follow. And this far spread Clamour so moves the greatest part of Mortals, as Antimony in these our Days is very ill spoken of, and no man dares put confidence in the Medicine thereof, which in it is found so various and unexpressible. [MEDICINE, NONE GREATER THAN IN ANTIMONY] For truly and holily I affirm (as truly as GOD is the Creator of all things visible, which are contained in Heaven or Earth, which either have come, or in time to come shall come unto our knowledge) that under Heaven, or by the Rays of the Sun, with the Guidance of Experience, can be found or demonstrated no greater Medicine, than is in this Mineral; yea, there is no Subject, in which so fluently and abundantly can be found such most certain Remedies for Health, as shall be declared (by sure and undeniable Experiments) to be in Antimony.

Son, attend to this my Discourse, and do thou Reader give heed to my Writings, and do you wise men of the World diligently observe my Declaration of Antimony founded on Experience. For my Theory ariseth from Nature, and my Practice proceeds from certain Experience, which shews its manifold Utility, and infinite Ways produceth the same, not without the incredible Admiration of all men. But I assent to you, and confess (as I have before acknowledged in my Writings) that Antimony at first is meer Venom, and before Preparation hath nothing in or with itself, but Poison; and that I affirm to be true. [DOCTORS REPREHENDED] But you, whosoever you are, insignized or not insignized with the Degree of Doctor, Master, or Bachelor, whether skilful in Art, or by some other privelage promoted; you, I say, who so inconsiderately and so arrogantly without Truth exclaim, and prate against me, pause a while, and forget not your own Argument, hear what I have to say. Antimony is Venom, therefore every One must beware he use it not. No, that doth not follow Mr. Doctor, Bachelor, or, Master; it doth not follow, I say, Mr Doctor, although you be proud of your Red Hat. Treacle is made of the most perillous Venom of a Viper, which is called 'animal', whence also it had its Name; therefore no man must use it, for there is poison in it. Doth this Consequence please you? How doth this my Doctrine like you? [NO GOOD IN ANTIMONY FOR THE HUMAN BODY, WITHOUT PREPARATION] You hear, that after Preparation, no Venenosity is found in Antimony; for by the Spagyric Art Antimony is converted from Venom into Medicine, no otherwise than as of the Venom of a Viper is said, which is converted into Treacle; but without Preparation you shall find no Good in it, nor anything of Medicinal Help, but much loss and detriment.

[VULCAN, MASTER AND REVEALER OF ALL SECRETS]

Now, whosoever desires to become a Disciple of Antimony, he must, after Prayer, and an earnest Invocation of GOD, betake himself to the School of Vulcan; for he is the Master and Revealer of all Secrets. [VULCAN, CONDEMNED BY WHOM] This Master is condemned by the Wise Men of the World, set very light by and derided; because they, by reason of their own Negligence and Malignity, have learned nothing of him; and all Revelation, through their own Sloath, is impeded: [MEDICINE, NOT PREPARED WITHOUT VULCAN] for no Medicine was ever prepared without Vulcan, whatsoever those senseless mad men shall babble and affirm to the Contrary.

[ANTIMONY, ITS WONDERFUL VIRTUES]

But I will proceed to the Proceed and Preparation of Antimony; for I little value the Clamours of arrogant and self applauding men: let them make and bring to light any Work that can excel Antimony. It is well known to me, that of Antimony may be made Medicines equal to Those, which are in gold and vulgar Mercury (I except the Astrum of Sol) for of this may be prepared Aurum Potabile against the Leprosie, of this may be made Spirit of Mercury, the highest Remedy against the French POX, of this other infinite Remedies may be prepared. If those Condemners cannot perceive and understand this, what wonder is it? None, because they have not learned it. No man can give a sound Judgement of that, which he never learned. [DESPISERS OF ANTIMONY COMPARED TO AN ASS] Let the Ass, an Animal like them in stupidity be their Example, who cannot teach a Shepherd how to handle his Pipe, so as to play an Harmonious Tune; because he hath not learned. So, right Judgement, with a solid Foundation cannot be given by a man, who before hath not bent his Studies that way, that from Writings he may be able to discern what, in such a Business, is just or unjust. [DOCTORS REPREHENDED] After the same manner in this Faculty, what can be attributed to any of the Doctors, before he hath from Writings, and by his own proper labour acquired Knowledge?

[VENOM, WHENCE IT ARISETH] Yet before I pass to the Process itself, some One may perhaps interrupt and ask me, which way both Minerals and other Things receive their Venenosity? What Venom is? Whence the Poison of every Thing hath its Original? How it may be taken away, also how such a Mineral may without peril securely be used for Health after evacuation of that Venom? To these Questions I will briefly and clearly answer. The Infusion of Venom falls under a twofold Consideration, viz. Natural and Supernatural.

[GOD'S END IN PROPOSING VENOMS]

The First Reason, why GOD the Supreme Lord of the Stars, and the maker of Heaven and Earth, hath proposed to us open Venom, especially in Minerals, is, that by this his Ordination he might show to us his Wonders and powerful Works, for distinction of Good and Evil, as in the Law he prescribed to us the Knowledge of That, which lies as a Duty on us to do, viz. to Choose the Good and Eschew the Evil. So also the Tree of Life in Paradise was proposed; its right use tended to Good, but its abuse brought the Fall to Evil; for by that GOD's Command was broke, whence proceeded Destruction and all Evil. This is the first Reason.

A Second Reason is, that by this we might comprehend and understand the Distinction between Evil and Good, and at length learn to exterminate Malice and reposit Goodness in its place. For GOD wills not, that man should perish and be destroyed, but that he should depart from Evil, and come to amendment of Life, that Destruction may be driven far away from his Soul. So, to Us his Creatures, with wonderful Conveniency hath he proposed Good and Evil, which is found both in the Precept of the Word, and in the Work of the Creature, that we may choose what is profitable and good for Health, and shun what is evil and pernitious.

Thirdly, Venom is also made by the Stars, when contrary Oppositions and Conjunctions of them happen, by which the Elements are Infected so, as they become the Cause of Pestilences, and other Venomous Diseases in this World: which also is to be understood of Comets.

Fourly, Venom is made from Things repugnant each to other, as when any One inkindles a deadly Poison in himself, by Anger or Sadness; also when a man drinks being above measure hot. Fifthly, among Venoms may be numbered Weapons, with which any One is slain; then the Abuse of Arms is Venom to that man. But when any One useth Arms, for the just and unblamable defence of his Body, to which end they were invented, then they may be accounted a certain kind of Medicine.

Lastly, the Cause of Venom may be demonstrated by Nature, in this manner: whatsoever Nature resists is Venom, and that because it fights against Nature. As when any one eats such Food, as his Stomach cannot bear, then that Food is Venom to him; for it is repugnant to Nature; on the contrary, if any One eat such Food, as is Friendly to his Stomach, to him that Food is Medicine.

But Venom is principally attracted to Bodies in the Earth, whilst they are a certain Mercurial Essence (now I speak of the Venom of Minerals) which yet is in an immature, crude, and not well digested Form, which is repugnant to Nature, and difficultly digeested; because such a Mercurial Essence is not yet perfect, well digested to Maturity, therefore it passeth through the whole Body, as a crude, immature, undigestible Mineral. As if crude corn should be eaten by men, that would be so difficult to be digested by the Stomach, as a notable debility of the Body would follow. For the natural Heat is too weak to deduce that to a due

Concoction and Perfection. Corn, which receives its Maturity from the Fire of the Great World, must afterward be throughly cocted by the Minor Fire, that it may be digested by the Microcosm. [CATHARTICKS, ALL VENOMOUS] As before we said, touching the boiling of Flesh to Maturity; so here the same is to be understood of Antimony, which being yet crude, and not throughly cocted in the Earth to fixedness, the stomach of Man (as I may so speak) is too weak to bear it, or retain the same, as by certain Experience is manifested, viz. that all Catharticks, whether Minerals, Animals or Vegetables, are venomous, because of a certain Mercurial volatile Matter still predominant in them; which volatile Spirit is the Cause why other things, which are in man, are expelled: [REMEDIES FIXED PURGE NOT] not that by this Means the Root itself of Diseases is laid hold on, which only is effected by the fixedness of every medicine. [ROOT OF DISEASES, HOW EXPELLED] For every Medicine throughly fixed, searcheth out fixed Diseases, and eradicates them; which Purgers not fixed cannot do, but they do only as it were carry away some Spoil of Diseases; or they may be compared to Water, which driven by force through a Street Penetrates not the Earth itself. [PURGING BY THE INFERIOR PARTS, NOT THE WAY TO EXPEL FIXED DISEASES] Fixed Remedies purge not by the Inferior Parts, because that is not the familiar way of Expelling fixed Venoms, and that way they would not touch the Kernel (as I may call it) or Center of the Disease; but by expelling Sweat, and otherways they strike at the very inmost Root of the Diseases, not contented with a certain superficial Expulsion of Filths. Therefore we often admonish all and every One, that all venomous Impurity is totally to be taken away from Antimony, before it can either be, or be called such a Medicine, as may safely be given. For this Cause, the Good must be separated from the Evil, the Fixed from the not fixed, and the Medicine from the Venom with accurate diligence, if we hope by the Use of Antimony to obtain true Honour, and true Utility; but Fire only can effect that. For Vulcan is the sole and only Master of all These. Whatsoever the Vulcan in the Greater Orbe leaves crude and perfects not, that in the Lesser World must be amended by a certain other Vulcan, ripening the Immature, and cocting the Crude by Heat, and separating the Pure from the Impure. That this is possible no man doubts; for dayly Experience teacheth the same, and it is very apparent in the Corporal Aspect of Colours, which proceed from the Fire. [FIRE, THE SEPARATOR OF VENOMS] For by Separation and Fire, which perfect Fixation, Venenosity is taken away, and a Change is made of the Evil into Good, as we have already said. Therefore Fire is the Separator of Venom from Medicine, and of Good from Evil; which is a thing, that None of the Physicians either dares or can truly and fundamentally own, or demonstrate to me, unless he who hath firmly contracted Friendship with Vulcan, and instituted the fiery Bath full of Love, by which the Spouse, being throughly purged from all Defilement, may legitimately lie down iwth her Bridegroom in the Marriage Bed.

Fie upon the Acuteness of the Worldly Wit of those, who neither understand, nor are willing to endeavour to understand these my Writings. if you did know, what is called fixed, and what not fixed, and what it signifies to separate the Pure from the Impure, assuredly you would purposely forget many Things, and omitting other vain Works, would follow me only. [ANTIMONY, SPEAKS OF ITSELF] For in me (Antimony speaks of himself) you will find Mercury, Sulphur and Salt, then which Nothing is more Conducible for the Health of men. [MERCURY, SULPHUR, AND SALT IN ANTIMONY] Mercury is in the Regulus, Sulphur in the Red Colour, and Salt in the remaining black Earth. He that can separate these, and again unite them in a due manner, according to Art, so as Fixation may bear Rule, without Venom, he may rejoice with Honour and Truth; because he hath obtained the Stone of Fire, which may be prepared of Antimony for the Health of Mortals, and for Temporal Sustentation with particular profit. [ANTIMONY, CONTAINS ALL COLOURS] For in Antimony you may find all Colours, Black, White, Red, Green, Blue, Yellow, and more other mixt Colours, than can be believed, all which may be separated apart, and known particularly, and singularly applied to use; according as the Artist intends, such an Ordination is to be instituted.

[ANTIMONY, ITS WONDERFUL VIRTUES] Therefore now will I distinctly declare, how Medicine is to be prepared, Venom to be expelled, Fixation to be set about, and a true Separation to be made, by which the Evil may be subdued and depressed, and the Good triumph and be taken into use. In the meanwhile, let the Lover of Art consider, that every of the other Metals may be compared to every of the Precious Stones; but this only contains universally the Virtue of all Stones; which those Colours, which it gives forth and exhibits to the Sight from itself in the Fire, do sufficiently demonstrate. Its Transparent Redness is assigned to the Carbuncle, Ruby and Coral; its Whiteness, to the Diamond and Crystal; its Blue Colour, to the Saphire; Green, to the Emerald; Yellow, to the Jacinth; its Black, to the Granate, which Stone contains in itself a a certain Blackness occultly absconded. But as to Metals, the Black is assigned to Saturn, the Red to Iron, the Yellow to Gold, the Green to Copper, the Blue to Silver, the White to Mercury, and its mixture of various Colours is attributed to Jupiter. [ANTIMONY, CONTAINS ALL COLOURS] But as all the colours of all Metals and Precious Stones are clearly found in Antimony; so also all the powers and Virtues of Medicine are no less showed in it, than the Colours aforesaid: but to educe from it all these Colours is not the Labour of one man. For our Life is circumscribed with Limits more straight, than will permit one man by his Labour throughly to learn whatsoever Nature keeps concealed and absconded in her bosom, in one certain way of Preparation, from Antimony by distillations is drawn forth an Humour acid and sharp, like true perfect Vinegar. Another way is prepared a shining Red Colour, sweet and savoury, as purified Honey or Sugar. Another way, a Wormwood like Bitterness proceeds therefrom; otherwise, a certain Acrimony, like some Salt-Oil: thus always one Nature follows another. Against, but Sublimation it is driven to the Olympic Mountains, like a flying Eagle, red, yellow and white. Also forced down by Descent, it yields diverse Colours and Preparations: also by Reverberation, of it is made a Metal, like common Lead. Likewise a transparent Glass, red, yellow, white, black, and endewed with other Colours: all which notwithstanding, are not safe to be used in Medicine, unless they be first proved by another Examen. Also it is reslved into rare and wonderful Oils, which are various and manifold, some of which are made perfect with Addition, others without mixtion of any other things; some likewise are taken inwardly, others only outwardly applied to common Ulcers, and Wounds. It supplies us with so many several Extractions, varied with so many Colours, as it would tire a Delphian Apollo to describe them all; but indeed, all the Mutations of its Nature, which are discovered through the Gate of Fire, it by its own Oracles will best unfold. [MERCURY, MADE OF ANTIMONY] Of it is made living Mercury, and Sulphur which burns like common Sulphur, so that of that Gunpowder might be made. Of it is made a true and natural Salt; and many other things are prepared of the same.

Therefore we begin to speak of the Preparations thereof, as of its Essence, Magistery, Arcanum, Elixir, and particular Tincture, in which you must imploy all diligence and Care; especially when I shall in my Writings declare to you the Stone of Fire, and its Preparation, together with other various Secrets and Arcanums, which indeed are scarcely at all known to the World; and which have been little regarded, since the Egyptians, Arabians and Chaldeans died, who professed these Arts: of which notwithstanding the use is very great, for searching out the very Fountain of true Medicine, and all other Works pertinent thereunto.

Now diligently mind, and with profound Meditation consider all the following Preparations, one succeeding another, as I shall reveal them. For there is no One inserted, which hath not its singular Utility, but every of them is useful, according as ordained as its State. A fixed Medicine of Antimony, expels fixed Diseases and eradicates tehm; but Antimony is not fixed, as when it is crude and not prepared, opens and purgeth the Stomach only, but toucheth not the Root of the Disease. Therefore I will set about the Preparation of all, that appertains to Antimony, and discover all the Keys of its Preparation, which now (as by a New Nativity) are brought to Light, and revealed by Fire, in the same state to which tehy were ordained by GOD their Creator. This unlocking and preparing of Mineral Antimony is performed by diverse Methods and Ways, by the disposure and governance of the Fire, with manifold labour of the Hands, whence proceeds the Operation, Virtue, Power and Colour of the Medicine itself. And since Antimony to the Aspect presents a crude black Colour, mixed with a little whiteness, I will first speak of its destructive alteration, which consists in Calcination and Incineration, and that is thus made.

[CALCINATION OF ANTIMONY]

Take Hungarian or other Antimony, the best you can get, grind it, if possible, to an Impalpable Powder; this Powder spread Thin all over the bottom of a Calcining Pan, round or square, which hath a Rim round about, the height of two Fingers thickness; set this Pan into a Calcining Furnace, and administer to it at first a very moderate Fire of Coals, which afterward increase gradually: when you see a Fume beginning to arise from the Antimony, stir it continually with an Iron Spatula, without ceasing, as long as it will give forth from itself any Fume. If in Calcining, the Antimony melt, or concrete into Clots, then remove it from the Fire, and when cold again reduce it to a subtle Powder, and as before calcine it, continually stirring as we said, until no more Fume will ascend. If need be repeat this Operation so often and so long, as until that Antimony put into the Fire, will neither fume, nor concrete into Clots, but in Colour resemble White and pure Ashes: Then is the calcination of Antimony rightly made.

[GLASS OF ANTIMONY, SIMPLE]

Put this Antimony thus calcined into a Goldsmiths Crucible set in a Furnace, and urge the Fire with Bellows, or put it into a Wine-Furnace, administering such Firee, as the Antimony may flow, like clear and pure Water. Then, that you may certainly and infallibly prove, whether the Glass made thereof be sufficiently cocted, and hath acquired a transparent Colour, put a long rod of Iron cold into the Crucible, and part of the glass will stick to the Iron, which with a hammer strike off, and hold up against the Light, to see whether it be clear, clean and transparent; if so, it is well, and perfectly mature.

Here let my Reader, unlearned and but a Beginner in Art, know (for I write not to men skilled in this Art, who have often experienced the powers of the fire, but to Candidates, Tyro's*, and the studious Disciples of the Spagyrick Science; because to make Glass of Antimony is a thing common, and well known to many) know, I say, that every Glass, whether made of Metals, Minerals, or any other Matter, must be thoroughly cocted in Fire to due Maturity, that it may have a clear and transparent Colour, and be apt for further Preparation to Medicinal use: which translucid and pure Maturity Vulcan only effects in his secret and hidden Nature. Therefore, let every man know, consider and retain this.

*Rightly doth Basilius say, he writes to the Tyro's of this Art, because he begins with the Glass of Antimony, that is, from the very Rudiments of Chymistry, and so accurately teacheth to make that, as no man how ignorant soever can be deceived therein: yet the Ancients have not seldom experienced, how often they have erred in the Praxis, for such I have written these Commentaries. For me, let every One please himself in his own Writings: surely I think I have offered somewhat, which Posterity will always thankfully accept. For although I did for several years most diligently read Basilius and other Masters of the Art of Arts, *and in Labouring following them, as exactly as possibly I could, yet I committed so many Errors (the rememberance of which fills me with Horror) lost so much Money, and was so often constrained to amend those Errors with labour, as I have compassion of all Those, who would enter into this way, incited thereunto by their earnest desire to help their Neighbours: for I have no respect to Others, who aim at nothing but Riches, and would make so noble an Art subservient to Avarice, the worst of all Vices; let them sustain the dammage they deserve to suffer. But do you, who are endued with a more noble Spirit, First seek the Kingdom of GOD, which is either constituted or propagated by Charity to your Neighbour, and all other Things, which other men so impiously seek, shall spontaneously (which is the bounty of GOD) be added to you. I need to use no great Arguments to persuade any man to read those Commentaries; for every One's own Business will sufficiently admonish him, when he shall see me often with one word, and a most simple Animadversion to save him so great Charges, which he hath too frequently bestowed in labouring without success. I do here candidly profess to thee, studious Reader, had the Manual Operations been as sincerely showed to me, as I here open them, I should have saved a great Sum of Money; for I very often erred, when I would over eagerly prosecute certain Processes of others, and by that vain endeavour, lost some Thousands of Florens. Yet I seldom twice repeated any of those Operations, which out Author (most sincerely and openly, of all that I know) hath in this Book inserted. I shall not here institute a Tyrocinium of Chymistry, as other Authors, well known to young Beginners, have already done; but I am willing, by Admonition to help those, who long since could loose this Subject from its Bonds, and with most fervent desire design to arive to the Goal exposed to their Eyes and Mind, least either slippery Blood in the Way, or Entellus now lying prostrate, should hinder them from gaining the proposed Reward, which is Riches and Health.*

When in the Method we have taught, you Antimony is converted into Glass, take a Platter or Dish made of Copper, which is smooth and broad, heat it hot at the Fire, otherwise your Matter will flie out; then pour in the fluid Matter as thin as you can, and you will have pure, yellow, transparent Glass of Antimony. This is the best way of preparing Glass of Antimony per se, without addition; and this Glass, above all others, is endewed with the greatest Virtue and Power, which it manifests after its further Preparation. This is by me called Pure Glass of Antimony.*

*This is now the Common, and well known way of making Glass of Antimony, which is profitable in many Operations: but to administer it so to the Sick without Distinction, is a Work full of danger and peril. It indeed succeeds happily, but this casual or accidental health of some, is not of so great moment, as therefore to expose the Life of one man to Peril. For I have seen a Sick man, who after he

had taken but half an ounce of the Infusion, vomited and purged above measure, and soon after died. [DOCTORS REPREHENDED] hence are those Tears, hence those Clamours arise against Chymists, as if the impious rashness of some false Chymists were to be imputed to the Art, which PseudoChymists care not how many Houses they fill with Funerals, provided one or two that are healed will blaze their Fame, and they can hear themselves called Doctors, and rob the simple of their money. The reason of this great danger is, because all the Emetick force of Antimony contained in the fixed Salt thereof, in which resides all its Venenosity, which weak Natures cannot overcome, and therefore receive not so much good from the Salutiferous virtue thereof, as hurt from its Venom. But this thing should not deter sound men from the use of Antimony, since they see it, even then when mixed with Venom, often to produce salutary Effects. They should rather thus reason; if that salutiferous Virtue be freed fromt he Noxious faculty, what Good would it not do, or what Diseases would it not heal? Therefore, behold I here offer to you such Glass of Antimony, as I myself use often, and may be used by every man, without any danger of a mortal Catastrophe.

Take pure Glass of Antimony, made as Basilius here teachet, melt it in a Crucible, and keep it in flux so long, as until a third part be consumed. Then let it cool, and grind the same to an Impalpable Powder, upon which pour Spirit of Wine highly rectified, until it stand three fingers above the Powder; close the Vessel firmly, and circulate the Matter for three Months; then by Distillation abstract the Spirit of Wine, or if it be tinged with Redness, (which always will be, if you have rightly operated) only pour it off, and keep it apart; for it is an excellent Medicine. The remaining Body put into a Crucible, permit it to flow, and then cast it into what Forms you will. For it can assume whatsoever Shapes you will have it, which may be set in Rings, and worn on the Hand. But its Medicinal use is thus.

Put this Glass for one Night in two ounces of Cold Wine, and in the Morning let the Sick drink that Wine, and you will find very good success, for it purgeth kindly, and if Nature incline to bring the Matter upward, it performs that action moderately, causing gentle Vomits. Only Note this: the prescribed Dose must be diminished, according to the Strength, Age and Constitution of the Sick. Here, Reader, candidly accept of this my first Admonition offer to thy self, and expect to find more, if you willingly and intently peruse the after following.

[GLASS OF ANTIMONY WITH BORAX]

For there are other Glasses prepared of Antimony, by Addition of Borax and other things, in this manner.

Take of Crude Antimony one part, of Venetian Borax two parts; put these together into a Crucible, which setting the Vessel in a Wind-Furnace, or urging the Fire with Bellows, cause to flow, that they may be well and perfectly mixed together, afterward pour out the Mixture into a Pan, or Dish of Copper made hot, as thin as is possible, as before was said in the Superior Preparation, and you will find you Antimony fair and transparently clear, *like a Pyropus or Ruby, provided you observe the due and accurate Method, Operating as you ought, in the Governing Fire.

*The Caution, to which our Author here ascribeds the Success, is that you use a most strong Fire, such as is required for melting Gold: for without this you cannot acquire the Redness of a Pyropus.

The Redness may be abstracted from this Red Glass, with Spirit of Wine*, and by long continued Circulation in Fire, be perfected, and rendered a most excellent, profitable and efficacious Medicine.

*Not with common Spirit of Wine, but with Philosophic Spirit, which for extracting this Tincture, I thus prepare. Take of Sal-Armoniac thrice sublimed four ounces Spirit of Wine, distilled upon Salt of Tartar so, as it may be perfectly dephlegmated: put them together in a Phial, which place in heat of Digestion the Spirit may fully imbibe Sulphur or Fire of the Sal- Armoniac; then distil the mixture by Alembic thrice, and you will have a true Menstruum, wherewith to Extract that Redness from the Glass of Antimony. Also the Tincture of this Glass is extracted with its proper Vinegar, and by a further Operation is perfected, and becomes a most excellent Medicament.

But a transparent white Glass of Antimony, after commixtion thereof, is prepared in this manner.

[ANOTHER GLASS OF ANTIMONY WITH BORAX] Take Antimony beat or ground small one part, Venetian Borax very pure four parts: put these, well mixed together, into a Crucible, and cause the Mixture to flow well. At first indeed it will be yellow, but if it stand longer in Fire, the yellowness vanisheth, the Matter receives a white Colour, and thenceforth becomes a fair and white Glass. Whether this colour be brought to perfect Maturity, you may prove with a cold Iron, as above is said. Many other ways, of Antimony may be formed Glasses* consisting almost of infinite Forms.

*Let him who desires to prepare more Glasses of Antimony, consult Beguinus, Hartman, Crollius, and other Authors; we here acquiesce in these proposed by Basilius.

But since my purpose here was not to describe other Glasses, then I myself had experienced, and which manifest happy success in Healing, I judged it unnecessary to waste Paper in describing them, or by a tedious discourse to weary the Reader; especially since, unto you is already in part proposed the principal Colour (viz. the Red) which is found in Glass made of Antimony. The black Colour, which Antimony had before Preparation, is now in a Spiritual manner flown up the Chimney; because in such a Spiritual manner, very much of the Venomous Substance had left it before, through the Expulsive force of the Fire, as by Calcination. Yet because in this Preparation all the whole Venom is not taken away from the Glass of Antimony, but it still retains very much thereof; I am willing (now I have begun) further to reveal to you, which way the Venom may wholly be removed from this Glass, and another Separation of the Pure from the Impure, of the Venom from the Medicine, be instituted; by which the Tongue of the Orator will be loosed, and occasion given to him of largely expressing my Praises, and publishing the same, as with a great Sound, through all Parts of this Inferiour Orb: which will be a necessary Consequence of the Gratitude of my Disciples, when they shall see with their Eyes, touch with their Hands, and with their Understanding comprehend, that I do their great profit, have declared to them the very Truth, without Deceit, and made them the Heirs of a memorable Testament.

Therefore the first Separation of the Sulphur from its Body, and the Extraction of the Tincture from its Salt, is performed in this manner. Take pure Glass of Antimony, as I taught you to make it, without the adjunction of any other Thing, Grind it to subtle Powder* impalpable as Flower;

*What I here shall advise is short, but very profitable, without which what the Author appoints cannot be done, nor by beating or by grinding in a Mortar can you ever bring the Body to a requisite fineness, much less upon a Porphyry Stone can you grind the same. Therefore first beat it in a Mortar, afterward mix it with distilled Vinegar, that it may have the Consistency of a soft Paplike matter, and so grind it upon a Porphry Stone, as Painters grind their Colours, and undoubtedly you will obtain your desire.

Which powder put into a Glass with a Plain flat bottom, called a Cucurbit, and there pour upon it strong Vinegar well rectified: then set the Vessel in a Digestive fire, or if it be Summer, expose it to the Sun, stiring it twice or thrice* a Day, and so long digest it in that temperate heat, as until the vinegar contract a Yellow Colour inclining to Redness, like the colour of most clean and well purified Gold.

*Thou art happy, if thou canst be wise by my Dammage, O Love of Art. I exactly followed this short Admonition, stirring the Cucurbit twice or thrice a Day, but the Matter was always coagulated like a Stone, and stuck so firmly to the bottom, as it could by no force be removed thence; but afterward, being more *wary, from the first I began to stir the Matter with a Wooden Spatula five or six times a Day, or oftner; you may imitate the same, if you be wise, not only here, but also in the Superior Preparation of Antimony, and in every Extraction of Tincture from Antimony.*

Then pour off this clear and pure Extraction, and pour on fresh Vinegar, and repeat the Operation, as long as the Vinegar is tinged, and until no more Tincture can be extracted. Filter all these Extractions mix'd together, and put them into a Glass Body, with its Head annexed, and by B.M. distil off the Vinegar; until in the Bottom remain a Yellow Powder, inclining to Redness. Upon this Powder pour distill Rain-water often times, and as often distill it off again, still pouring on fresh distilled Rain-water. Repeat this labour so long, as until the Powder remain Sweet and *grateful.

Our most sincere Author here deceives you not, but conceals a certain manual Operation, which if you attend to me clearly discovering the same, the Work itself will never fail to Answer your desire. If you have much Tincture, you must have a great Cucurbit; if Little, a less will serve. For if you take a greater Vessel, than your Tincture requires, the vinegar must necessarily have a great fire to cause it to ascend, by reason of the height it must unavoidably rise, or it cannot be distilled; and in sustaining so forcible a Fire, there is great danger of Corrupting the Tincture itself. Here also is required another Caution; viz. this, after two thirds are distilled off, you must change your Vessel and put the remaining Matter into a less Glass body, and thence distill off the Vinegar, until the Remanency acquire the just thickness of a Poultis. Also take heed, as Basilius seems to intimate, that you distil not off the Vinegar unto dryness, lest the Tincture by Adustion be wholly corrupted.

Notwithstanding all This my own Precaution now given, I could not choose, but labour a whole year to little purpose, often repeating this Tincture with a vain endeavour, whence I was almost as often weary of Chymistry through desperation; for my Tincture was of no efficacy in Medicine; because a meer Caput-Mortuum only, unsavoury and of no value. Hence consider how little any Process profits, whether set down in Writing, or received from a Friend by word of mouth, unless you set to your hand, and practically learn every particular of the Work fit to be observed in operating. Also see, how liberally I deal with you, in revealing that, the ignorance of which hath put me into great trouble and charge. The manual Operation, which is requisite for edulcorating this Pap-like Matter remaining in the bottom, is this. Upon this Matter pour distilled Water, and gently abstract the same by Balneo. When you have repeated this a third time, you will find the Water to come off sweet; which time must be observed and with very great diligence. For if you be deceived in that, your work is at an end, all your labour lost, and you shall get nothing, but a Caput Mortuum. For as soon as twenty, or at most thirty drops of sweet water come forth, an Acidity appears again and distils forth, which the unwary judging to be an Acidity of the Vinegar formerly added, proceed in distilling, expecting the Water to come forth sweet; but this being the Acidity of Antimony, which (the Vinegar being extracted) immediately follows the Sweet Water, that persisting to distil destroys the whole Virtue of the Antimony, and leaves nothing remaining but an unsavoury Caput-Mortuum. Therefoer be thou more wary, and as soon as this Sweet Water comes forth, cease to distil, and take out the Pap-like Matter residing in the Bottom, and putting that into another Glass, permit it to dry at the Solar-Heat; or else evaporate all its Moisture with most gentle Fire, that it may remain a dry Powder: and when you have avoided this danger, then go on.

[TINCTURE OF ANTIMONY, FROM ITS GLASS]

This Powder grind upon a Marble or Glass, first made hot; then put it in a Glass Body, and pour upon it of the best rectified Spirit of Wine, so much as will stand above it three Fingers thickness: then set it in a Digestive heat, as above, for extracting the Tincture of Antimony, which will be high coloured and pleasantly red to amazement; and it will deposit a certain Earth, or feculency in the bottom.

This Extraction is sweet, grateful, and so very efficacious in Medicine, as no man, that hath not experienced the same, will give credit thereunto. The Feces in the bottom retain the Venenosity, but the Extraction Medicine only, which Experience hath taught to be profitable Remedy for men and Beasts. For if three or four Granes of this Medicine be taken, it expels the Leprosie and Gallick Lues, purifies the Blood, drives away Melancholy, and resists all Venom: and whosoever labours with Shortness of Breath, Difficulty of Breathing, or Pricking of the Sides, he may be cured by the Use of this Medicine: *which effects many wonderful Things, if rightly administered, and in due time.

These Medicaments, which perform their Operations, not by sensible force, as Catharticks, Emeticks, Diaphoreticks, and the like are wont to operate, but insensibly uniting their own more pure Universal Spirit unto our Spirits, amend Nature and restore it to health, are not to be used, unless where the Body hath first been cleansed from the impurities of pecant Humours, otherwise you cast these Peals into a Dunghill, where (overwhelmed with Filths) they cannot shine and manifest their Virtues. For although, by reason of their manifold Virtues, they may be called Universals, yet they are to be numbered with Topicks, before which Generals are to be used, according to the opinion of Galen, and all Physicians.

The Tincture here spoken of, performs all those Cures, which Basilius mentions, if the use of it be continued for some time. For where that Saying is of force, Medicines used help, continued heal, it must certainly be applied to those especially, which insensibly operate.

That Yellow Powder, of which mention is made above before it is extracted with Spirit of Wine, may be ground upon a hot Stone, and then put into Eggs* boiled hard, in place of the Yolk, which is to be taken out: set these Eggs in a moist Place, or Cellar, and the Powder will resolve into a yellow Liquor.

Indeed soft Eggs, according to the Saying; are always warily and softly to be handled; but in these hard Eggs also, I have somewhat to advise you of; for if after you have taken out the Yolk, you be not mindful to break that Pellicle, which divides it from the wHite, you will wonder to see how your Balsom will intrude itself within the White, and deprive you of a great part thereof.

This admirable Liquor heals all green Wounds, if soon after a Wound is made, it be put therein with a soft Feather, and the Wound well covered with a Styptick, or other Preservative Playster. All fresh Wounds inflicted either by Prick or Cut, are healed by this Liquor, without Putrefaction, Inflammation, or any superfluity of Filth, so perfectly; as unto him, who created Heaven and Earth, and in them insited such a Medicine, due Thanks and Praise deservedly ought to be given. In all old, malignant, and corrosive Wounds, use this Extraction or Balsom of Antimony, and it will never fail Thee in thy necessity. And thou thy self, after me wilt write an Encomium of its Praises and publish the Virtues thereof, by which extrenally applied miserable Mortals may be made happy: for the Wolf and *Cancer yeild to it; Rottenness in the Bones, malignant Ulcers corroded and perforate with Worms fly from it, and it restores to pristine Health, and provides Entertainment for that with itself, when its fixedness shall be duly used inwardly, and other Convenient Means duly applied outwardly.

If Chirurgions would here give credit to our Author, with how great Care would they prepare this Balsom for themselves, and with how great Fruit, and how frequently might they use the same? For I interposing my Judgement must say, that Basilius here comes far short, in expressing its due Praises; for it performs more, than he declares of it. [HISTORY OF THE VIRTUES OF BALSOM OF ANTIMONY] One short History, drawn from the Centuries of my Medicinal Observations, will confirm the truth of what I have said. A certain Woman, about forty Years of Age, for seven years together suffered great dolours in her left Breast, which were accompanied with a Tumor and Hardness. Those Chirurgeons and Physicians, who she advised with, did all with one Consent judge her Disease to be a Cancer; and she was also judged to labour with a Cancer, by the Censure of that famous Practitioner, who at Orscotus (a Village about the Dukes-Wood) very laudably and happily practised Chirurgery, and drew to himself a vast number of People: for after he had, for three Month together, in vain endeavoured to heal this Disease, he severely pronounced her Breast was to be cut off, or the Disease could not be extirpated. The woman, resolving rather to suffer all Dolours of the Disease, then to sustain so cruel and inhumane a Remedie, came to me. I, beholding her Breast, found it wholly inflamed, and twise as big as the other, and an abundance of thin Humours flowing to the Wound. I purposed to try all I could do, rather than suffer this miserable Woman to perish; and thinking of this Balsom resolved to try, whether That, which in other Diseases had fulfilled the promises of its Author, would fail me here. Therefore, to the Diseased Woman waiting my Answer, I said; in eight days time I would resolve her, whether, there was an hopes of Cure or not, without Cutting off; and thereupon gave her this Remedy to anoint her Breast therewith: and which is very strange, in the Space of two Days the Matter came to Ripeness, and a just Consistency. Therefore, I then filled with good hope, adjoined inward and outward Remedies, which seemed convenient for the purpose, and in two Months Space the Womans Breast was perfectly healed. Upon this I, not without a perculiar Joy, blessed and praised the Lord, that had conferred so great virtue on this Balsom.

[OIL OF ANTIMONY, FROM ITS GLASS BY DISTILLATION]

Also Glass of Antimony is by me two ways reduced to an Oil, in distillation (as they call it) by Alembeck.

Take Glass of Antimony; as it is made of the Minera of Antimony, subtily pulverized, and extract its Tincture with distilled Vinegar; afterward abstract the Vinegar thence and edulcorate the remaining Powder. Then pour on Spirit of Wine, with which extract the Tincture, and circulate it in a Pelican well closed, for an entire Month. Afterward, distil it per se, without any Addition, with a certain singular *Dexterity; and you will thence receive a wonderful grateful and sweet Medicine, in the form of a Red Oil, of which after may be formed the Stone of Fire.

*This is the Work, this is the Labour, very few true Sons of Art (whom Apollo loves) could extract this Tincture by Alembeck. There is need (as Basilius saith) of a certain peculiar manual Operation. This Tincture I sought many years, and at length (GOD favouring me) found the same. [OIL OF ANTIMONY, ITS PREPARATION ENIGMATICALLY DESCRIBED] Wilt thou have me discover it to Thee by an Enigma? I see thou desirest I should, therefore take this Mystery, thus. Alciatus, painting a Dolphin wreathed about an Anchor, write these words: Make not too much hast. Esteem of this Admonition, not only in all your Life, but also in this very matter, as very profitable to you: for the hasty Bitch (as the Saying is) brings forth blind Whelps. Therefore I again and again admonish you, to cause Wings to be prepared for your Matter, by Juno, Bacchus and Vulcan; but as you love your Life, permit it not suddenly to flie, rather deliver it to Mercury to be instructed by him gradually to accustom itself to flying; yea, bind it with a Cord, lest (as a Bird got out of a Cage, and past your Reach) it through Ignorance approach too near the Sun, and with Icarus, having its

Feathers burnt fall headlong into the Sea. But after you have detained it for its due time, loose its bonds, that it may fly, and come to those fortunate Islands, unto which all Sons of Arts direct their Sight, and where unto all Adeptists aim to arrive, as unto their desired and long sought Harbour. Here, O Lover of Art, you should not be offended, or angry with me, as if I deluded you (desirous of the Knowledge of this Secret) by a Tantalick Apple shown. What should I do? I in this Case give you advice. Would you have me cast Pearls before Swine? and unto all men expose the Mystery, which the Ancient kept so holily, and might not reveal it, unless to the worthy Sons of Art only? Thou thy self wouldest bewail nothing more, and wouldest even execrate me, for doing so. They, who understand me, understand Art: and unto such as are Chymists, have I opened the way, which if they diligently travel in, they may arrive, where they desire to be. No man did ever so clearly reveal this to me; but by reading the Writings of Authors, strenuously labouring, and trusting in GOD without fainting or desperation (which is a most efficatious kind of Prayer) I at length attained to what I have. Do thou study, and be diligent, that thou mayest comprehend: for he, who, knows how to render Tinctures volatile, is already admitted into the very Penetrale, and Conclave of the Chymical Art; because of all other Mysteries the Method is the same. Peruse the Fables, search into the Riddles, and consider the Parables of all wise men; they all tend hither, and all say the same. Compare the Parables of others, with this my Enigma, and this with them, that you may understand how much Light I have added in all, and how Easy I have made the way to those serene Temples of Wisdom.

[QUINTESSENCE OF ANTIMONY, WHAT]

This Oil is the Quintessence, and the highest, that can be written of Antimony; as you may find in my former Writings, wherein I have made a short Declaration of Antimony, and in which I showed also, that there are four Instruments required for its Preparation, and the fifth is that, in which Vulcan hath fixed his Residence. Understand thus: four Preparations must be made before it can be perfected; and the fifth is the Utility, and effect of the Work in the Body of man. The first Labour is Calcination and Liquefaction into Glass. The second is Digestion, by which Extraction is performed. The third is Coagulation. The fourth is Distillation into Oil, and after that Separation follows Fixation, by the ultimate Coagulation, through which the Matter is deduced to a perlucid Fiery Stone; which that it may operate upon Metals, must be fermented, for acquiring its penetrative Property; but not so much, as that Ancient Stone of the Philosophers, because it is not Universal; but only tingeth particularly. Touching which, about the End of this Book, more shall be spoken when we treat of the Stone of Fire.

This distilled Oil* of which we have now spoken, effects all things, that are necessary to be known by a Physician, and which he hath need of, in his Cures.

*Had I not known Basilius, I should have thought him, in this place to have dealt like a Deceiver, or Vagabond Medicaster with you: but the Matter itself unto me, so often speaks for him, as I religiously scruple even in the least to doubt his Promises. For whatsoever I have experienced (but there are very few Processes contained in this Book, which I have not tried: for He, from the very first, was my Teacher, Friend and Patron) I have found so very efficacious beyond the Authors Promises, that it seems to me, he hath been sparing in declaring the virtues of his Medicaments, least in praising them, he should be thought too much to commend himself. Yet I shall not here in his stead, undertake comment much on their laudable Virtues. Let him who believes not, make trial, that he may know. Whosoever shall by his own incredulity be deterred from experiencing the Truth hereof, he will suffer punishment enough for his Offence, by the Want of the fruit of the same. For this Oil, if rightly used in its time, is a Medicine truly Universal. Consider, I pray, what I say, if rightly used in its time, that is, the Body being firsted purged from gross and crude Humours, and general Medicines used (as you may remember I did before admonish) this Oil is an Universal Medicine, for healing all Diseases Curable. For Chymists are not so mad, or conceited, by reason of the Goodness and Virtue of their Medicaments, as not to judge some Diseases to be Unsanable. Who can restore any of the Prnicipal Members absumed by putridness? yet I would not have all Diseases judged unsanable, by these our Chymical Remedies, which are everywhere vulgarly condemned as such. As for Example, how often have I restored the Crystalline Humour taken away; which who judgeth not impossible to be reduced? But, of these and the like, another place will be more fit to write. Only of this Medicament I say, that it heals Feavers of every kind; yea, even the Quartan itself (that ancient Reproach of Physicians) and in Chronical Distempers manifests wonderful Effects. Here among many of my Observations I will give you one only Experiment. [HISTORY OF DROPSY CURED] In the Year 1665. A young Maid, aged twenty one Years, swollen to an enormous grossness with the Dropsie, came to me for help. I took this only for her Medicine. For I gave her no other thing, then this very Medicament twice a Day, to which I dayly added a Clister: and in twenty days she had sweat so much, as her Body was lessened half. Within that space of twenty Days, as I said, she also voided of Urine (provoked by the same Medicament) not a little, but her Sweat was wonderful.

Note: me Friend, and Lover of Art, that this Oil, whether you prepare it yourself, or receive it from antoher prepared by him, doth not imitate other Diaphoreticks in operating, which being used, will in their first Dose provoke Sweats. For if this be given to a Patient whose Body is obstructed with Humours, the first Dose acts nothing, but gently opens the Passages, that Sweats may be procured; the next day it causeth a gentle and kindly breathing of Sweats only; the third Day it Sweats moderately; but the fourth Day, and thence forward, it causeth such an aboundance of Sweat, as the Waters proceeding thence run *through the Bed upon the Floor. here is need of a true Physician; Hercules Club will profit little, if not in the Hand of Hercules himself.*

[THE QUINTESSENCE OF ANTIMONY, ITS WONDERFUL VIRTUES]
The Dose of it before Coagulation is eight Grains taken in Wine. It makes a man very young again, delivers him from all Melancholy, and whatsoever in the Body of man grows and increaseth, as the Hairs and Nails, fall off, and the whole man is renewed as a Phoenix (if such a feigned Bird, which is only here for Example sake named by me, can anywhere be found upon Earth) is renewed by Fire. And this Medicine can no more be burned by the Fire, than the Feathers of that unknown Salamander: for it consumes all Symptoms in the Body, like consuming Fire, to which it is deservedly likened; it drives away every Evil, and expels all That, which Aurum-Potabile is capable to expel. The *Astrum of Sol only exceeds every Medicine of the World when rightly prepared to perfect Fixation: for the Astrum of Sol, and the Astrum of Mercury arise almost from the very same Blood of their Mother, and from one original of vivifick Sanity.

Let no man here prodigally or rashly wast his own Gold, now he hears of the Astrum of Sol, nor expose himself to so great Hazard, as to enter a perillous Combat with vulgar Mercury. In the Chymical World another Sol shines, and another Mercury attends on Jupiter. Yet the Chymical Sol, or Mercury here, is not Gold, but more excellent than all Gold; yea, more potent than every Mercury, although fabulous, and feigned to be capable to restore the Dead to Life: it is the Gold, and Argent-Vive of Philosophers, which Basilius here hints at. But we have treated, and must treat of Antimony only.

Now, no man hath cause to fear, that this Oil of Antimony Extracted first with distilled Vinegar, and afterward with most pure and subtle Spirit of Wine, and then further exalted (as highly as possible) by Vulcan, will in any wise purge, or excite frequent Stools, or make any Alterations: for it effects nothing of all this, but by Sweat, Urine, and Spittle, expels the very Root of the Disease to amazement, and restores whatsoever is corrupted by any Symptom.

But Common Glass of Antimony, being ground to Powder, put into a little Wine (viz. six Grains or more of the Glass, according to the strength of Nature) and that mixture set in heat for one Night, and in the Morning the Wine* poured off clear from the remaining Powder, and so drunk by the Patient, purgeth downward exciting several Stools, and oftentimes also provokes Vomiting, by reason of the Mercurial immature Property, which is yet inherent in the Glass, as every intelligent Physician will easily judge, and indeed he ought to further to Examine how this Glass, when he would purge with it, ought to be provoked, and administed in a due Dose.

*This is a Common Vomitory, or Emetick Wine, well known, which all wandering Empiricks now use in all Places, sometimes with a prosperous, sometimes with Contrary, always ambiguous Success; which proceeds partly from the Physician and partly from the Medicine. [HISTORY OF GEORGE CASTRIOT] This is a Thing to be bewayled; for as histories relate, that George Castriot King of the Epirots, when the Emperour of the Turks had often asked him, how his Sword, which he had sent, when Peace was made, according to his agreement with the Turk, could perpetrate such wonders as he spake of, saying he saw not anything singular in it, made this Answer: I did indeed send the Sword of Scanderbeg, but not Scanderbeg's Arm, with which that Sword was managed, so as to perform so great Miracles: so, very many Chymical Medicines, are either dead, or (which is more to be deplored) oftentimes the Causes of Death, when not managed by the hand of a skilful Doctor. Which unhappy Success of this Medicine is caused from the Mercurial Properties, with which it is too much impregnated (as Basilius well notes in this Place) and which I am wont to correct in this manner.

Take Glass of Antimony, more pure, four ounces. Venetian Borax one-half ounce. Melt them together. This being artificially done, you will have a Green Glass transparent as Emerald. Grind this to a subtle Powder, upon which pour French wine, and permit the mixture to stand for several days in Moderate Heat.

Of this Wine give to the Sick, from one drachma to two ounces, according to the Age, Habit of Body, Strength, and other Things either Natural, or not Natural, which the Prudence of the Physician (when he sits as Judge, whether the Life of any One is likely to be continued or not) ought always well to consider. That is Emetick Wine may be given to the Sick without peril, Experience the most certain Mistress of Physicians hath taught me, and yet more than this: for when the Wine poured in the Powder shall be all exhausted, if you pour on more French Wine, that will also be imbibed with the same Virtues. For here Antimony discovers in itself to be somewhat, that is of all wonderful Things the most admirable: because it contains in itself inexhaustable Treasures, and although you take from it, yet you diminish not the Virtues thereof. A like stupendous Miracle also is in extracting the Vinegar of the same, and in other Works fit to be kept under the seal of Harpocrates.

Many men are required for the Searching out the Powers and Virtues of this Subject. For I alone, by reason of the shortness of my Time, could not dive into and search out all things, do you thy self set about the Work, and after me, yea with me, thou wilt praise me and I thee: if you find out anymore; I praise you by these my Writings, and shall commend you out of the Sepulcher to which I am destinated, although in Body thou art to me unknown, nor ever had I any discourse with thee, because perhaps not yet born.

[OIL OF ANTIMONY MADE ANOTHER WAY]

Common Glass of Antimony is also by Addition distilled into a laudable and salutary oil, which may be used without peril, with very great profit in the Epilepsie; as here following I shall teach.

Grind the Glass of Antimony to as subtle a Powder as possibly you can, then put it into a Glass-Vessel with a flat Bottom, and pour upon the Powder the Juice of unripe Grapes, then having well luted hte Vessel digest it for certain Days. This being done abstract all the Juice; afterward, grind it well moistened with Spirit of Vinegar, and a double Weight of clarified Sugar. Then, having put it into a Retort, in the Name of the Most High begin to distil, and at last administer a vehement Fire, and you will acquire a most Red Oil; which must be clarified unto Transparency with *Spirit of Wine.

*When the Author saith, it must be clarified with Spirit of Wine unto Transparency; the Admonition is short indeed, but of great weight. For he wills, that this Oil should be driven over by Alembeck, the signification and manual Operation of which, I have already above taught.

The Use of this, given in a small Quantity, is found to be most profitable. With this Oil Spirit of Salt may be joined, and the Mixture poured upon a subtle prepared Calx of Gold, (which how it should be made I have already taught in other of my writings) which hath before, together with its Water, passed by Alembeck. If this be done, this Menstruum take to itself the Tincture* of Gold only, and leaves the Body untouched.

*Do you think, O Lover of Chymistry, you understand what you read? You cannot understand, unless either divinely Philip, or humanely Oedipus, appear to you, and clearly teach you the way of preparing this Tincture. The difficulty of the Enigma consists in this; viz. that all Menstruums, with which Tinctures are extracted, must necessarily be void of Colour; otherwise how can you know: whether you obtain the Tincture you would extract, or only retract the same you poured on? I will not detain you with a tedious Discourse full of ambiguities, but lead you asi t were by the hand, showing you how I instituted this Process in the Year 1665. If you thence, by your attention, and comparing the precedent with the present, and these with thsoe that follow, reap any profit, open the Bosom of your Heart, that no part of this may fall to Earth.

I took that Red Oil, thus far prepared as is already showed, and rectified it by Retort; and then acquired a White Oil, of an acid but grateful Taste. Upon this I poured half so much Spirit of Salt: the Mixture I digested in a Phial for a full Month, that these two Spirits might be well conjoined; afterward, for the better conjunction of them, I distilled them thrice by Retort. Then I poured them upon the Calx of Gold (the Method of preparing which you will find in other Writings *of Basilius) and set them together in Digestion for a Month; which being elapsed, the Menstruum was tinged with a deep Yellow Colour inclining to redness. I leisurely poured off the Tincture, and having put it into a Retort, with gentle Fire abstracted the Humidity, that a red Powder might remain in the Bottom. This Powder I edulcorated with distilled Water, and again extracted the Tincture with Spirit of Wine; then I rendered this Dragon volatile, and gave him his own Tail to be devoured for six whole Months, and obtained a Tincture most pleasant and grateful; ten or twelve Grains of which given to the Sick, provoke Sweat, comfort the Natural Powers, and (not to amuse the Intelligent words) in all Diseases both of Humane and other bodies, it is an universal Medicine.*

Since it hath happened to me here to make mention of the most excellent of all Tinctures, I will once teach the Chymist what will be of use to him for the future. That is to say, it is of great concern to know, with what Menstruum every Tincture should be extracted, For it is not sufficient (according to the erroneous Opinion of many) that Menstruums be sweet and void of Corrosion; but it also behooful, that there be in them a peculiar Amity and Conveniency with the Mercury of the Body, on which they are poured, that from the same they may extract its true and sincere Sulphur. By Example, I shall teach you somewhat more clearly. Distilled Water extracts the Tincture from Sulphur, made of the Glass of Antimony by distilled Vinegar. But if in this Operation you persuade yourself you have separated the Pure from the Impure, you will be deceived: for this Water imbibes a certain Salt, which infects the Tincture; but Spirit of Wine rectified is its proper Menstruum: because That only assumes the volatile Sulphur thereof, and hath no Commerce with the Salt.

The same happens in Tincture of Corals, which is extracted with Spirit of Wine distilled upon Orange Pills: for here you obtain not the sincere Tincture of Corals; because, by this Menstruum, the pure Sulphur is not separated from the Body of the Corals. The like Error to be committed in many other Things, I have observed by Experience, which should be esteemed the best Mistress, unless we take it for granted that chargeable and fruitless Processes are necessarily required in this Art. But that I may conclude with the Tincture, whence all this Discourse hath proceeded; I would have no man to think this to be the Aurum Potabile of Philosophers: for this would be a very great Error in Philosophy, and give occasion to Sophisters (as their manner is) to prefer their Sophisms before the Truth itself. Though this Tincture is most precious, and a Tincture of Gold, yet it hath only assumed the Colour of Gold: but the weight thereof, which is proper to Aurum Potabile, adheres not thereunto.

Touching the potable Medicine here is not place of speaking, unless I would trangress the limits, which I have at this time prescribed myself, of Commenting upon the Triumphant Chariot of Antimony, which our Basil Valentine hath made for it is so truly magnficent. Otherwise, I should declare, how sol might be prepared by Venus and Vulcan, so as in the space of two hours to resolve itself into Mercury united with Bacchus, leaving very few feces; which Mercurial Menstruum may again be separated from the resolved Gold; and so you might acquire a most grateful Liquor very ponderous, which can never afterward be reduced to its former Consistence. This very Operation I have showed to some Curious Lovers of Chymistry. But of these elsewhere another Occasion of Writing will be given.

[LABOUR, NECESSARILY REQUIRED]

When the Fermentation is made, I shall have need of a vast Quantity of Paper to declare all the Arcanum's of Nature, which by this Medicine are effected beyond the Opinion of all men. I urge this so much the more earnestly to the Physician, that he may consider those things which I propose Philosophically, betake himself to labour, perform this Preparation of Antimony, and deduce it to Use; then, he himself will dayly find more Praise, and learn from it more Operations than any of the other Physicians could have prescribed him.

When you shall have brought Antimony so far, and duely perfercted your Work, in which you are to act prudently, and the matter is to be largely and profoundly weighed, that by Labour you may acquire Experience; then may you boast that you have obtained the Magistery, which is known or communicated to few. This Magistery mix'd with a solution or Tincture of Corals, and exhibited with Cordial Water effects Wonders in Diseases, that are to be cured by purifying the Blood. And whatsoever Distemper is offered to you, in which the Blood is corrupted by any Accident, this Magistery heals it, exhilarates the Heart, promotes Chastity and Honesty, and renders man apt and fit for everything he takes in hand.

For all these Benefits to the Creator and Conserver of all Things, thanks is always to be given from the bottom of our Heart; because he hath with so great Compassion respected his Creatures, Infirm both in body and Mind, and supplied us with Means, by which the Diseases of either may be healed, and we in every necessity obtain solace, assistance and perfect Help.

Now my Intention is to proceed, and speak somewhat of the Arcanum of Antimony, but with very great Brevity.

Take of Antimony most subtlely pulverized One Part, of Sal Armoniack*, so called, which is brought from Armenia,

Of Antimony and Sal-Armoniack equal parts are to be taken, which Basilius seems to intend, but I know not how he forgot to mention it.

also pulverized; mix these, and putting them into a Retort distill them together,*

That with one and the same labour, the Sal-Armoniack together with the Antimony, may be distilled and sublimed, such an instrument, as this I here show you, describing all its Parts, may be made.

A.. is the Furnace. B. the Retort. C. the Recipient. D. the Aperture wit ha Pipe of a Moderate bigness, on which may be set the Alembeck E. The other Furnace is F, which containing a Moderate Fire, sublimes what falls into the receiving Vessel up into the Alembeck E. And so the Matter which is distilled from Retort B, by the Fire of the Furnace F, is presently sublimed; Which may not only be useful in this Case, but also in every Sublimation of other Matters.

and upon that which comes forth in the Distillation pour common distilled Rain-water, but let it first be made hot, and so by edulcorating remove all the Salt, that no Acrimony may remain, and the Antimony will appear like pure, white shining Feathers. Dry them with subtle Heat, and having put them in a Glass circulatory or Pelican, pour on them good and perfectly rectified Spirit of Vitriol, and Circulate the Mixture till both be well conjoined* and united, then distill the whole, and pour on Spirit of Wine, circulate again; then let seperated be made, and remove the Feces settling to the Bottom, but keep the Arcanum which remains mixt with the Spirit of Wine and Vitriol.

This Union must be so firm, as in distilling one may not be separated from the other; otherwise you will lose your Labour and Cost. Of how great moment this Union is in Chymistry, they best know, who only by confounding two things together, think they shall effect wonders; but afterwards (their Experience failing them) they learn how great difference there is between Union and Confusion: for Things confounded receive no Virtue, that was not in them before; but by Union, I know not what Spirit is ingested, which performs such things as the Mind of man could never perceive to have their being thence.

Hence consider in the Generations of Animals (who would believe it!) how from the Union of Elements is generated Sight, Taste, Touching, and so many Powers of Animals, which are insited in none of the Elements, and yet arise from them united. Whensoever it happens, that any Tincture seems to have united itself with its Menstruum, and afterward may be separated therefrom, that therefore is because Matrimony is not legitimately Celebrated, nor the union in a due manner perfect; which you shall more than once see to happen in the Tincture of Sol and Antimony.

The Instrument, by which conjoin my Tinctures, and am wont to copulate them in an undissolvable Copulation, you shall find described hereafter in this very Book. That in Spirit of Wine is to be noted, which happens not in other Menstruums; because it is most easily united to Things, and again with a slight artifice separated from the same.

Now when you again rectify this Arcanum, one drop of it exhibited with Rose water, is more available than a Pot full of the Decoction of Herbs; for it causeth a good Appetite, corrects the Stomach, and concocts all malignity in it, drives away Sadness and Melancholy, makes good Blood and a good Digestion; in the Suffocation of the Matrix and Cholick Passion (both which it wonderfully appeaseth) it is instead of a Treasure of inestimable Price and deserves Commendation, not easily expressible by Words.

[ELIXIR OF ANTIMONY]
After the Arcanum of Antimony next in order follows the Elixir* of the same, which you may prepare in this manner.

*This Process as it is easy to perform, so it may by us be easily passed over, lest we should seem to take Pen in hand, rather from an itching desire of Writing, then for illuminating Things obscure.

Take, in the name of the Lord, good Minera of Antimony, grind it subtlely, and sublime it with half so much Sal-Armoniack. Whatsoever shall be sublimed put into a Glass retort, and thrice distill it, seperating the Feces everytime. Afterward remove from it the Sal-Armoniack by edulcoration, and reverberate the Matter of Antimony in a Vessel well closed, with moderate Fire (not forcing too much) until it become like the Earth of Cinnabar. This being done, pour on it strong distilled Wine Vinegar, and extract its Redness; afterward abstract the Vinegar, until a Powder remain. This abstraction must be made in Balneo. Then, extract this Powder with Spirit of Wine, that the Feces may be separated, and you will have a pure and clear Extraction. Having finished this Operation, put this Spirit of Wine together with the Extraction into a Cucurbit, and add thereto a little of the Tincture of Corals, and of the Quintessence of Rubarb, and then administer the Dose of three or four Grains.

It causeth gentle Stools, and purgeth without Gripings of the Belly; and indeed if you have proceeded well in preparing, it renders the Blood agile, and is a Medicine apt for those who desire Gentle Purgations.

Here perhaps some Physician may wonder, how 'tis possible, that this Medicine should cause moderate and easy Purgations, when as Antimony is a Matter vehement and forcible, and to it is joined Rubarb, which of itself also hath a Purging Property. But let him cease his admiration, and know that the venomous purging power of Antimony is by this Preparation so mortified, as it can apprehend or expel nothing; but as soon as some purging Simple is adjoined to it, it then according to the powers of its own Nature performs the Office of opening and purging. But Antimony prepared hath no action upon the *Stomach, thence to expel its impurities; but by the purging Medicine, its adjunct, acquires a more open Field, and therein can operate without Impediment any other way, and discern, yea search out the way of Effecting that better, to which it was ordained and prepared, without hindrance.

[CARTHARTICKS EXPEL BUT CORRECT NOT] Note here very seriously, that Galenick Catharticks have power of expelling, but not of Correction Humours; but Chymical Purgers are endued with either Faculty; and certainly it should not be minded how much is expelled, but how much is healed, which the occult power of Medicaments prepared Chymically doth much better effect, than that common and publick violence of purging forcibly.

[ELIXIR OF ANTIMONY, ITS VIRTUES]

I would have all men to credit these words, since I have no necessity to write other than the Truth. This Elixir in such manner prepared, as I have taught, penetrates and purgeth the Body, as Antimony purgeth Gold, and frees it from all Impurity: So that if I would at large commemorate all the powers and virtues thereof, I must put up my Supplications to the GOD of Heaven, and intreat him to vouchsafe me a longer Life, that I might laud his wonderful Works, and search out further, and according to Verity communicate to others what I have found, that they with me excited to admiration, may publickly render thanks to their Creator, for his so great Blessings.

But to proceed in my purpose, having once begun, I here describe the Virtues of Antimony, as far as I have experienced them; yet what is hid from my knowledge, I ought to pass over in silence. For it becomes me not to give my Judgement of things unknown, and which I have not with myself experimented, but I leave them, commending the same to other Judges, who with study and labour in this Subject, have made some good progress. No one man can be so expert in knowing the Virtues of Antimony, as nothing shall remain unknown by him, not only by reason of the shortness of his Life (as I before said) but also, and chiefly because some new thing is dayly found in it.

[ANTIMONY YET CRUDE IT FATTENS SWINE, HOW]

Therefore, let men know, that Antimony not only purgeth Gold, cleanseth and frees it from every peregrine Matter, and from all other Metals, but also (by a power innate in itself) effects the same in Men and Beasts. If a Farmer purpose in himself to keep up and fatten any of his Cattle, as for Example an Hog; two or three days before, let him give to the Swine a convenient Dose of crude Antimony, about half a dram mix'd with his Food, that by it he may be purged; through which Purgation he will not only acquire an Appetite to his Meat, but the sooner increase and be fattened. And if any Swine labour with a Disease about his Liver or other Parts, or else be Leprous, Antimony causeth the Leprosie to be dryed up and expelled.

[WHY AUTHOR INDUCED RUDE EXAMPLES]

This Example seems indeed to sound somewhat gross and rustical, to the Ears of Great men especially; but my purpose in proposing it was only to the end, that private Men and Laicks, whose Brains were not by Nature fabricated to the most subtle Philosophy of the Learned, may see the Truth hereof, in the very Operation itself, with their own Eyes; also that by this rude Proposal, they might give greater credit to my other Writings, in which I have spoken a little more subtley of these Things. Yet I would have no man, following me as his Author, to give a Medicine of Crude Antimony to men; for mute Animals can in their Stomach concoct much more hard Foods, than the tender Complexion of Men is able to digest. Wherefore, he who would rightly and with profit use Antimony, he must learn the Preparation thereof first, and afterward know the Dose, as what is convenient for the Young, and what for the Old; how much may be given to robust Bodies, and how much to the weak, in which no small Mystery of this Art consists, the ignorance of which will do more hurt than an imprudent Physician can do good.

[ANTIMONY DIVERSELY PREPARED HATH DIVERSE EFFECTS]

Should I confirm all things by Examples, that would be the Cause of a very Prolix Writing; therefore I will break off this Discourse, and pass on to another Preparation of Antimony, and describe its fixedness; which acts like Wine, from which its Spirit is substracted and separated from its Body. [WINE HEATS, VINEGAR COOLS] This Spirit heals the Body internally, and if externally applied, draws to itself all the Heat of a part inflamed: but, on the contrary, when of the Wine, Vinegar is made, it cools, either inwardly or outwardly applied; although the Wine and Vinegar have their Original from the same Root, and proceed from the same Stock. The Reason of this diversity is, because Vinegar is made through digestion only, by which Putrefaction of the Wine follows, together with a Vegetable Fixation: but on the contrary, Spirit of Wine is made with Separation by distilling, or vegetable subliming, which renders the Spirit volatile. By like reason Antimony is prepared, and according to its diverse Preparations hath diverse Effects, and diversely communicates its Gifts to us, which are scarcely comprehensible by the humane Intellect. But the fixedness thereof, touching which I here treat, is thus prepared.

[POWDER OF ANTIMONY, FIXED]

Take of Antimony as much as you will, grind it to a subtle Powder, which put into a Cucurbit, and pour on it of Aqua Fortis so much as will stand above it the breadth of six Fingers; and having well and firmly closed the Vessel, place it in a subtle heat for ten Days, that the Matter may be extracted. Decant off this Extraction pure and clear, and filter it, that it may be freee from all feculencies and Impurities; then put this Extraction into a Glass-Body, and abstract all the Aqua Fortis by Distillation in Ashes or Sand, and in the bottom the Powder of Antimony will remain yellow and dry. Upon this pour distilled Rain-water, and put it in a like Glass in moderate heat, and you will have a Red Extraction. This again filter, and gently distil off the Rain-water by B.M. and the Powder will remain red in the Bottom. Upon this red Powder pour strong distilled Vinegar: this Vinegar will in some time draw to itself the Colour red as Blood, and put down Feces. Afterward distil off the Vinegar, and there will again remain a red Powder. This Powder reverberate continually for three days together without ceasing in an open Fire; This being done, abstract the Tincture from it by Spirit of Wine, and separate the Feces remaining from the Tincture. All these Works being with so great labour performed, again separate the Spirit of Wine by distillation in Balneo, and a fixed *Red Powder will remain, which operates wonderfully.

*Diaphoretick Antimony is sold in Shops, but what here the Author shews us, by the name of Fixed Powder of Antimony, is not to be bought for Silver or Gold; the Virtues of which so far exceed all that, of which the Common sort are Partakers: In vain with so great attention and study (of which in preparing this Powder, there is very great need) did our Philosopher intend this Work, if these Mysteries of so great Effects must come to the handling of the Vulgar, or be publickly sold for Money. Let him who attains to this fixed Powder use it in Chronical Diseases, especially where Sweats are to be excited, and he will see Effects causing him to rejoice, if he use it in himself; and by which he will be glorified, if he use it in others.

Half a dram of this being taken thrice a day, viz. Morning, Noon, and Night, or oftner, hurts no man; for it expels all clotted Blood out of the Body, and being long taken securely opens all perillous Imposthums, and expels them; radically cures the French Disease, causeth new Hairs to grow, and notably renovates the whole man.

[FLOWERS OF ANTIMONY]

Now, since I have taught to make a fixed Powder of Antimony, and the Extraction thereof very commodious for Use, leaving this Discourse, I purpose briefly to treat of the Flowers of Antimony, which may be many ways prepared. But the greatest part* of men neither can discourse of, nor answer to these; because they have not learned the Processes of such Operations: but the least part, viz. the Disciples, Apostles, and Followers of the Spagyrick Art, will more esteem my Writings, more diligently read them, and more prudently give Judgement of the same.

*How much Chymistry was impeached by Calumnies, in the times of Basilius, is manifest by the very many Reliques of Writers, with which some Theologicians, imprudently judging what they understood not, and Politicians (not much more prudent than them) have defamed their own Books; and in the mean while also given occasion to Others, more throughly searching into the matter, of judging *those very Authors, with not greater circumspection to have likewise bespattered other innocent Persons with their Censure. I do not here speak of those Writers, who sharply reprehend certain Vagabond Sophisters, that covering their own Wickedness, under the Pretext of a most noble Art, do by a great Name impose great Frauds upon the People. For this kind of men are not only worthy of severe Reprehension, but also of due Punishment. But, what Evil do they deserve, if under their Denomination the Good be abused? Why is the most certain and so salutary and profitable an Art proscribed? Because there are men found, which use not the Art itself, but the Name and Shadow of this Art. Yet I am unwilling to prolong this Apology, lest Envy, which hath been the greatest cause of Calumny, fall upon me in this manner lamenting, whilst I hear Basilius encouraging his, and have reason to applaud our own Times, in which some part of that most thick Cloud, which cast out so many Thunders, is already vanished. [CHYMICAL MEDICINES SOLD IN SHOPS] In Shops they now sell Medicaments, Chymically prepared (as they say) and those very Persons, who are willing mostly to be esteemed Hippocratick Disciples, scarcely dare to condemn Chymistry, and since they call into use what are made by the Chymical Art, they cannot deny it. Are not those Times at hand, in which Elias the Artist, the Revealer of greater Mysteries is to come? Of whose coming Paracelsus so clearly prophesied in carious places in his Writings? Perhaps it will be worth our while, for the Solace of the oppressed Disciples of Basilius, to quote certain places, in which he predicts the coming of Elias not then born: which is any One commodiously interpret, as all other Sayings of that man are to be taken, he will find nothing of absurdity in them, unless he resolve to discover his own absurd Stupidity, or wicked Envy. In the Book of Minerals, Chap 8. Paracelsus thus writes: what is the most vile, GOD suffers to be discovered, but whwat is of greater moment is yet hid from the Vulgar, until the coming of Elias the Artist; others read, until the Art of Elias, when he comes. And again, in his Book of Minerals, Treatise the first. It is indeed true (saith he) that many things lie hid in the Earth, which I, as well as others am ignorant of. For this I Know, GOD, in time to come will manifest his Wonders, and bring to light many more of them, then unto this Day have been known by us. Also this is true; there is nothing absconded, which shall not be revealed; therefore there cometh One, whose Magnale lives not yet, who shall reveal many Things.*

Therefore be comforted, be comforted, O Lover of Chymistry, and prepare the way of that Elias, who brings happy times, and will reveal more Secrets than our Ancestors, by reason of Envy, and the Iniquity of their Days durst discover. Whosoever thou art, conversing in this Art, confer some small matter to this felicity; and let us give the World that Medicine, which by reason of evil Humors predominant, it cannot take all at once, by degrees, that it may gradually recover of its Disease, and the Time of Elias come (for Arts also, as well as is understood of other things, have their Elias, saith Theophrastus) where it will be lawful for us to speak freely of these things, and openly to do good to our Neighbours, without persecution of the Impious. Read, understand, and comfort yourself with these.

But, my Disciple and Follower, if you will imitate me, my advise is, that you take up your Cross, at first, and suffer as I have suffered; learn to bear Persecution, as I have already born it, labour, as all our Predecessors with me have done; with continual Prayers seek unto the Lord GOD, and be thou patient, and laborious without weariness, and then the Most High, who hath mercifully heard me, will not forsake Thee: for this Cause I every hour give thanks to GOD, as my Eyes are filled with Tears can and do witness.

Now, to proceed in my Instruction, touching the Flowers of Antimony, it is to be understood, that the true Flores of Antimony, may be prepared, not one, but various ways, as is known to every Spagyrist. There are some who drive them, mix'd with Sal-Armoniack, over by Retort; then they edulcorate them, by washing away the Sal-Armoniack, and these they greatly esteem; for these Flowers are of a fair and white Colour. Others have perculiar Instruments for this Work, prepared with windy Caverns, through which the Antimony may receive the Air, and be sublimed. Others, setting three Alembecks one upon another sublime them with strong Fire, and with one and the same labour make white, yellow, and Red Flores; all which ways I have tried, and found no Error in them: but the Process, by which I make Flowers of Antimony, most profitable for Medicine, and more efficacious in their Operations is this.

I mixed the red Flowers of Antimony with Colcothar of Vitriol, and sublimed them together thrice. So, the Essence of Vitriol ascends with them, and the Flores are more strong: which being done, I extract the same Flowers with Spirit of Wine. The Feces settle to the bottom, and separate themselves from the Spirit. These the Artificer lays asie, and distils off the Spirit of Wine in B.M. until the Powder remains dry.

[FLOWERS OF ANTIMONY, THEIR VIRTUE]

These are my prepared Flowers of Antimony, which I administered to my Brethren, and others, who in there Necessities, required help of me, for their Souls spiritual, in respect of my Ecclesiastical State, and for their Bodies temporal, by reason of the Trust they reposed in my Art. These Flores purge gently, without frequent, or excessive Stools, and have cured many Tertian and Quartan Fevers, also very many other Diseases; so that I purposed, by the help of our Saviour Jesus, and his most Holy Mother Mary, to ordain in my Testament a perpetual Monument upon my Altar, of all the Cures which I have performed by his grace; that I might so doing, not only give thanks to GOD, but also make my Gratitude known to Posterity, that they likewise may acknowledge the wonderful works of the Most High, which I (by my diligence) have extracted from the Bowels of Nature, and which he himself had hid and absconde in her profound and most secret Recesses.

But touching the Sublimations of Antimony, which are afterwar called Flowers; let the Reader further observe, viz. that they are like Waters, which break out in high Mountains. Now, of the difference of waters, which arise in the highest Mountains, yea in higher than they, if such can be foun; for even unto them woul the waters ascend; since it is known, that in the tops of the highest Mountains, Springs do very often issue it; an of other waters which are foun by digging deep in the Earth, and by following their Springs must be searched out: [MATRIX PERCULIAR TO EVERY ELEMENT] any man may judge that the Matrix of waters in the Earth, is on one part more abundantly replenishe with the Riches of waters, then on another; since every Element hath a peculiar Matrix, either strong or weak, according as it is produced by the Sydus, whence Elements derive their Original an have being. Now, when such a Matrix is strong and potent in the Earth, it can drive forth its Seed strongly and efficaciously from itself, by a vehement Pressure, even up to the Snowy Mountains of the Alps, or to the very top of the Babylonish* Tower.

*This Parable is of very great moment, but so very clear to those, from whose Eyes the Cataract is taken away, as to explain it to them, would be to hold a Candle to the Light of the Sun: to others, from whose sight the Cataract is not took off, this place gives no occasion of detracting the same. Therefore, read, peruse, and meditate; Day is an Instructor to the Day; the later Reading explains the former, and the former the later.

If any fatuate man hear this my Discourse, he will say, I am either mad or drunk with Wine; but this will be no other than a Reproach, like to that, which was cast upon the Disciples of our Saviour. Of Sublimation, the Reason is the same; for as Waters, which are many times found in the highest Mountains, are more salubrious, and more cool than those, which by digging deep into the Earth are found in Plains: so, if the Matter by pressure & force of fire be driven upwards to the Mountains of the Ancient Wise Men, who died long before my time, the Earth, which for the most part is unprofitable, remains until its Salt shall be extracted from it for its proper use. Thus is made Separation, by which the Evil may be distinguished from the Good, the Pure from the Impure, the thick from the thin, the subtle from that which is not subtle, and the Venom from the Medicament. We miserable Mortals, by Death which we have deserved for our Sins are put into the Earth, until we putrefie by time, and be reduced to filths; and afterward by the Heavenly Fire and Heat raised, clarified, and exalted to a Celestial Sublimation, where all our Feces, all Sins, and every Impurity shall be separated, and we made the Sons of GOD, and of Eternal Life, unto which the Lord of his Mercy and Goodness bring me with you. But I hope no man will take amiss this Comparation of the Mundane with the Spiritual, viz. the Heavenly Exaltation with the Earthly Sublimation. For no man should suppose what I have done, to be done without Reason, but rather know, that I am not ignorant what is white or black, how much the tenebrous and dismal Air differs from the serene and clear Heaven. Therefore let us break off this Discourse, and produce another Preparation of Antimony.

Let the Disciple, Apostle, and faithful Imitator of Art, understand this Instruction, and according to the true Philosophick Doctrine faithfully consider, that every Extraction from Antimony (as also from all other Things) hath great difference in Operation, which neither consists in the Matter, nor is known by the Matter, from which it is drawn; but consists and remains in the Preparation, and in the Addition, by which the Virtue is extracted from the Matter, as is known by Experience; as for Example. Whatsoever is Extracted from Antimony, or any other thing with Spirit of Wine, hath a far other virtue of Operating, than those, which are extracted with good and sharp Vinegar. The Causes of this I have already hinted in my other Writings; but the principal Cause have is, because all Extractions made with Spirit of Wine, from Antimony, or any purging Herbs, Roots, or Seeds (understand of the first Extraction) powerfully expel by Seidge: but on the contrary, whatsoever is extracted with Vinegar, purgeth not downward but rather prevents that, and retains in a certain peculiar manner, by which the Volatile is changed into fixed. This is a singular Secret, and an Arcanum of great price; but there are none, or very few found, who mind such things; because many things are hidden, and lie deeply buried in this Arcanum, which no One, either Master or Servant, nor any Wise man of this World hath unto this Day observed or considered.

[EXTRACT OF ANTIMONY] Therefore the Extraction of Antimony is made two ways, viz. with Vinegar, and with Spirit of Wine. Vinegar obstructs, and Spirit of Wine, of itself powerfully expels and causeth Urine, as also Stools; as elsewhere in another manner is shewed, and especially where I speak of my Twelve Keys, as namely, that the Extraction of Glass of Antimony moderately purgeth; but on the contrary the Extraction of the same Glass, which is made with Vinegar purgeth not: which is true and not permixt with any falsity. But this Experience gives occasion of thinking and reflecting, by which way of Reasoning, Nature gives promotion and production to a true Philosopher. But it is a thing much to be admired, that every Subject, which is first of all extracted with Spirit of Wine, should have a Purging Property. Yet when Glass of Antimony is from the beginning extracted with distilled Vinegar, and that Vinegar again abstracted, and then the Antimony extracted with Spirit of Wine, all its venomous purging virtue passeth away, and no sign thereof remains, nor assumes it to itself any power of provoking Stools; but it performs its Operations by Sweat, and other ways, chiefly by Salivation and Ejection by the Mouth; it searcheth out all hurtful Evils in the Body, purgeth the Blood, heals the Diseases of the Lungs, and profits those who are strait-breasted, and troubled with a frequent Cough. In a word it Cures very many Disease, also asswageth a Malignant Cough, and whatsoever is of that Disposition, and is a Medicine very admirable.

Moreover, thre is another Extraction of Antimony made in this manner. Grind crude Antimony to powder, and pour upon it strong Vinegar, not of Wine, but made of its proper Minera, and expose the Mixture in a Vessel well closed to the Solar heat; then, after some time the Vinegar will be tinged with a Blood-like Colour, pour off this Extraction clear, filter it, and distil by Alembick in Sant: then again, in distilling, it shews admirable Colours, pleasant to the Sight, and wonderful in Aspect. This Oil* at length becomes Red as Blood and leaves many Feces and prevails against many Infirmities: [EXTRACT OF ANTIMONY, ITS VIRTUES AND USE] for its singular Virtue and Use is commanded in the Leprosy; the New Disease lately risen amongst the Soldiers is by it consumed and dried up, and indeed it effects Wonders.

*Here thy Sincerity, Valentine, is suspected. Who can by this thy Prescription make this Quintessence, which Petrus the Spaniard, in his Book of the Quintessence of all Things, deservedly extols, as the greatest Secret of Philosophy? What shall I say? Malice makes thee, not a perverse, but timerous man, fearing, lest if Arcanum's should be communicated openly to the wicked, they would do more hurt with them then good. This Process seems to me to be purposely described obscurely by this Religious Man (why else should he not have written otherwise!) because he knew the Sons of Art would understand it by his Prescript. But that you, Reader, may understand, you have not in vain spent your Money in buying, or time in reading these Commentaries, I will clearly and nakedly discover to you, how I myself have oftentimes performed this very Work: do you give good heed to all Things, that you may not at all be deficient; for the Operations are so concatenated, or co-linked together, as one being omitted, or negligently performed, all the other are spoiled, and your Labour cannot answer your Desires.

Take the best Minera of Antimony, which is friable)for if you take crude Antimony, as Basilius seems to indicated, you can effect nothing; because it hath already lost its most subtle Sulphur in the first Distillation) grind it to so subtle a Powder, as it may pass through a Tiffany Seive: put it into a Cucurbit, and pour upon it Vinegar, which according to Art is distilled from its proper Minera. Set it in Digestion for forty Days, and (if you have exactly observed all things, which are here unto required) your Vinegar will be tinged with a Colour red as Blood. This red Tincture poured off by Inclination, put into a Retort, and gently abstract the Vinegar. The Powder remaining extract with Spirit of Wine, that it also may contract a bloodlike Colour. Put this Extraction into a Circulatory Vessel, like to this, the Figure of which I here expose; because I never found any more apt to render the Spirits volatile: Then place this double vessel in B.M. to be digested so long, as until you see the Tincture raise itself upwards and pass over volatile by

Alembeck; seeing this, cool your Vessel, and put all the Matter into a Cucurbit, and distil the Spirit according to Art, which will pass over the Helm as red as Blood. Then again abstract the Spirit, and you will have a most ponderous, thick Oil.

How this Oil should after this be joined with its own Salt, and united, we elsewhere speak; the use of which in amending Metals is very great. Here we have described it, and brought is so far, as it becomes a most excellent Medicine in grievous Diseases, which are in all places accounted uncurable. It performs its whole Operation by Sweats. And since there is no Disease, which it helps not; what need is there to name any? It is better to be altogether Silent, then to detract from its praises, by reciting a few. There is no man who hath made any Progress in Chymistry, that knows not what the Quintessence of Antimony is.

The Physician before all Things, should diligently contemplate its use, according to his own Experience and Knowledge; but especially completing its Preparation in a due manner, without being weary of his labour, or forgetting any of those Things which are prescribed to be performed.

LIVER OF ANTIMONY]

Again, another Extraction of Antimony is thus instituted. Take, in the Name of the Lord, of Antimony and crude Tartar, of each equal parts; put these well mixed together in Powders, into a strong Crucible, which will not suffer the Spirits to penetrate it, and burn this Matter in the Fire, until the Tartar be wholly combust: this work must be done in a Wind-furnace. Grind this burnt Matter to a subtle Powder, and pour on that Common Water first made hot, and so edulcorate the Matter by Lixiviating. And so it becomes a Liver*, so called by many of our Ancestors, who lived long before us.

*The Liver is a Cause of much Discourse in Banquets, and the Liver of Antimony will be to us no small Occasion of the like in Chymical Operations. But in the first place consider, that instead of Crude Tartar, it is better to take Salt of Tartar, not only for accelerating the Operation (for otherwise it must be melted so long, as until the Tartar be changed into Salt) but chiefly, that you may have Glass of a far better Colour. Also Basilius forgot, or for some Reason did omit, to appoint the Glass first to be poured into a Platter made hot, and then beaten to Powder in an hot Mortar: otherwise the Glass, by reason of the Salt of Tartar, as soon as it takes the cold Air is changed into a certain Pulse or Pap. Besides, he omitted to determine the Quantity of Water, in which this Powder should be dissolved, that we may have a more fair and deep Colour; in which Exaltation of Colour very much is sited. Also the Precipitation of the Liver from the Water, which must be made with Vinegar, be involved in Silence; although this, and the above mentioned, are necessary in this Operation.

Here I am unwilling to forbear to admonish, that not only in this, but in every Melting of Antimony, the Artist ought to observe the Face of Heaven, and begin his Work when the same is clear and serene. If you do otherwise, you will in vain deplore the Obscurity of the Colour in your Liver of Antimony. For if you laugh at me, attributing much Virtue to the Influences of the Stars, I shall deride you, deploring the unluckie Success of many Processes. But I would not digress so far, as to take on me to prove the Virtues of Celestial Influences, against men, either knowing so little, as they cannot understand, or having experienced somewhat do not discern; but in the meanwhile are so obstinate, as they will not believe those things which they see, have tried, and in very deed found to be so. I would no more urge Reasons against these men, then against these, who deny even the Mutation of Metals by the Stone of Philosophers. We judge such men more worthy of Contempt than Refutation, who say that is not possible, which they have beheld with their Eyes, and done with their hands: for it is very rude to say, I deny, I deny, who proves? These perverse men by their thus acting, do sometimes provoke the patience of good ingenious Artists, judging that they, with a certain Zeal of confirming what they assert, will proceed so far, as to discover to them their Experiment of so excellent an Art. But I do not think that any of them, who have obtained the Mystery will be so imprudent, as unadvisedly to cast Pearls before Swine, and to discover to the unworthy, what GOD hath revealed to him; or give them of the Bread he Eats, which is not to be cast to Dogs.

Therefore, returning to the Matter from whence I digressed, I affirm, that there are some times of the year, in which if Liver of Antimony be made, and precipitated with a due Menstruum, it will be imbibed with altogether another Colour, and be endued with other Virtues than that, which is made at another time; and that, both for Metals, and for healing the Infirmities of men, as I my self have experienced in many grievous Diseases, and Symptoms of Diseases. I will also add this: from the Liver of Antimony may be extracted a Redness with Spirit of Wine, which Redness is made volatile, and passeth over the Helm, which also may be exhibited to all without danger. Nor is there any great need of that Caution of Basilius (even before the Redness is volatilized) that it must be given in a small Quantity. For being given from thirty to forty, or fifty Drops, it sweats moderately, and doth not Purge or Vomit: but it effects wonders in purging the Blood, extirpating the Roots of a Disease, and rendring the Patient vigorous, by insensible Expiration, and its occult Virtues. This Vendible Wine needs not the Bush of Eloquence to commend it to the Sick; who once having experienced its Virtues, know what it can do, and that it as much answers their Desires, as they esteem their Money.

Put this Liver dried into a Cucurbit, pour thereon most pure Spirit of Wine; abstract the Spirit by distilling in B.M. so that a third part only may remain. But before Distillation, the Spirit of Wine together with the Extraction must be filtered through Paper. This Extraction may indeed be profitably used; but in a small Dose, and with great Caution. What happens in this Operation is very admirable. For the Spirit of Wine abstracted, can no more be united with the red Extraction, whence it was distilled; but one floats above the other, as Water and Oyl, which cannot be mixed. But if the abstracted Spirit of Wine be poured upon other Liver of Antimony, it again attracts the Colour to itself; yet this, although poured upon the former Extraction, cannot be mixed therewith. Which is a Thing so strange, as it may be numbered among Wonders. But who can declare the Wonders of GOD? or who will worthily esteem the Gifts of the Creator, which he hath implanted in his Creatures? by us scarcely perscrutable with deep Meditation.

I before made mention of the Extraction of Antimony, from its Glass* by Vinegar, and also by Spirit of Wine: but I now say, when such an Extraction is made by Vinegar, and the Vinegar is again abstracted by B.M. and the Powder which remains is resolved in a moist place, into Oyl or Liquor of a Yellow Colour; it effects such Wonders in Wounds, new and old, as I neither can, nor dare to commit them all to writing.

*Here our Author acts as a Teacher careful, and full of Affection, who not satisfied once to mention, doth often inculcate the principal Precepts of his Doctrine. But, what it is, that specially moves him to repeat the Virtues of the Sulphur of Antimony, I see not: he saith, he repeats nothing in vain; therefore do thou, Reader, if thou judgest it of Concern, more attently consider, whether you may not here find somewhat that is not mentioned, or the Reason why it is again spoken of. I, who profess myself to write to the Intelligent, reiterate nothing here. He that comprehends, let him comprehend; he that hath not there understood, I fear will not here understand.

[LIVER OF ANTIMONY, ITS VIRTUES]

For it represseth all Symptoms of what kind so ever, suffereth none to take Root, and admits no Putrefaction in fresh Wounds. Also the Extraction of this Powder, before Solution is made by Spirit of Wine, effects the same, and yields not us inferior to other Medicaments, which are administered against internal Affects.

I have often made mention of this Preparation in other of my Writings, also in this Treatise of Antimony, very largely; because I know how great benefits and how great Secrets are latent in it. Therefore I hope, no Disciple will be affected with tediousness, by Reason of Repetitions in my Writings, which I faithfully open and bring to Light. For whatsoever I write is not without Reason; and my words are Short, but require much Consideration, although often repeated. To the Ignorant my Discourses contribute little understanding, to Children and the unexperienced little Profit; but to my Disciples and Apostles, much health and prosperity.

EXTRACT OF ANTIMONY, BY A CAUSTICK WATER]

There remains another Extraction by a Caustick Water, which Experience hath taught me in this manner.

Take of Vitriol and Common Salt, equal parts; from these by Retort distil a Water*, which being forced out by vehement fire, comes forth a matter like thin Butter, or the Sediment of Oil Olive, which keep apart for use.

*Here I will teach you the Manual Operation, O Lover of Chymistry, which undoubtedly you will greatly esteem of, when you shall find the great commodity thereof in operating. Lest, as it often happens, when you distil the Spirits of Metals, your Vessels should be broken. Of your Earth Retort A. open the upper hole B. into which put your matter by Parts, lest all together senting the heat, should act all to forcibly; and presently Close the Hole with its proper Cover. To the Spirits received in the Vessel C. exit is given by the hole D. into the other opposit Receiver E. to which again is applied the other Receiver F. So, the more subtle Spirits ascending through the Hole D. settle in the Recipient F. But the more gross remain in the bottom G. of the Reciever C. This Instrument will be most apt for your use here; not only, as I said, lest a most strong Spirit passing out break the Glasses, but also for other Works, as by an easy Speculation you will hence gather.

Subtly grind the Caput-mortuum, and in a Cellar permit it to resolve into Water, this Water keep and filter it through Paper. Afterward take Hungarian Antimony, grind it to a fine Powder, and having put it in a Cucurbit with a flat bottom, pour this Water thereon, and set the Vessel in Heat. When it hath stood there for a due time, the Matter will be like an Amethyst, with a blackish Violet-Colour. Then augment the Fire much, and you will have a transparent Colour, like unto a blue Saphire. From this Colour precipitate a white Powder, by pouring on Common Water. [EXTRACT OF ANTIMONY, ITS VIRTUES, AND USE] This Powder taken, hath the same Operation, as the red Extraction of Glass of Antimony, by Seidge, and it also excites Vomiting. [MARS TRANSMUTES INTO VENUS] In that Solution made from the Caput- Mortuum, and kept in a Cellar, if thin Plates of Iron be digested, Mars will be truly transmuted into Venus, as Experience will teach.

Now further consider. Take that distilled Oil or Water, as is spoken of above in this process and pour it upon Crocus Martis, with Sulphur reverberated to a Redness; set the Mixture in Heat, and you will have an extracted Tincture of Mars, red as Blood. Take of this Extraction one part; of the Red Extraction of Antimony, which is prepared with fixed Salt Nitre and Spirit of Wine, three Parts; of the Water of Mercury* leisurely injected through a long Pipe; one Part;

*[WATER OF MERCURY, HOW MADE] Chymists, that they may with the Ingenuities of their Readers; and more, lest any but the true Students of Art should penetrate into their Secrets, deliver not all Things in one place, but scatter

71

their Documents, that by the Diligent Collection of them, they may judge of their Aptness, as the Eagle proves her Young, exposing them to the Solar Rays: so you see Basilius here proposeth the use of Water of Mercury, which he taught to be made in his Treatise, which is called a Supplement, or rather gave a rude Draught of that Process. For neither there, nor here doth he make mention of an hole, that must be open, in the superior part of the Retort, and thereinto a long Pipe fitted through which the Mercury may be put in, in very small Parcels. For if you include a very small part of Mercury in a Retort, first made very hot with a vehement Fire, as this must be, if you would extract the Spirit, that Mercury, with its own vehement and untamable violence, would not only burst the Retort, but overthrow the Furnace also; unless you give it a larger space, and greater liberty of Flying; so that, after it hath visited many Retorts, it may rest, and being as it were tired, settle. But since it is well known to all true Chymists, of how great Virtue this Mercury is, in the Resolution of Metals, I will here make no further mention thereof.

and of the Calx of Gold dissolved in this Caustick Water, half a part. Mix all these together, and after they are canted off clear, distil the Mixture with a Moderate Fire in Sand. All will not pass over by Distillation, but a fair clear Solution remains fixed * in the Bottom; which we may use in old open Wounds, wherein it laies a Foundation for Healing to Amazement.

*This Solution is not yet fixed, but if you be not already wearied with labour, by a further Operation you may fix it. The principal Use of this is, in the Emendation of Metals, which Basilius doth not so much as mention. Now the Genius of all Chymists will understand me, here candidly discovering this Secret to all. Do thou, Lover of Chymistry, in mind and though swiftly follow me expounding the Oracle; but the Operation cannot be so swiftly performed.

This Powder must first be Extracted with strong Vinegar, which afterward abstract, and what remains in the bottom edulcorate with distilled Water: again Extract it with Spirit of Wine, and abstract the Spirit, and in the bottom will remain a Red Powder. Join this with the fixed Salt, which is made of the Feces, which remained after the Vinegar was used for Extraction. And deliver it to Vulcan for three Months space, that it may no more fly from the Fire, but most pleasingly sport with and in the same. If you perform this, you have Two conjoyned in an inseperable Matrimony: and you have separated the pure from the impure, have rendered the Volatile fixed, and fixed the Volatile, and are not far from that Felicity, which will answer all your Desires.

The Caput-Mortuum which is left, being resolved in an Humid place, yields a Liquor so sharp, as no Aqua Fortis may be compared with it in sharpness. But of these enough at this time. For I must now speak of a White Powder, which may also be prepared of Antimony in this manner.

[POWDER OF ANTIMONY, WHITE AND FIXED] Take pure Antimony, which is brought from Hungaria, or found in like Mountainous Places; grind it to a subtle Powder: take also the same measure of pure Salnitre, which hath been the third time diligently cleansed. This Composition burn in a new glazed Pot (which was never infected with Fatness) in a Circulatory Fire; not all together, but by parts, and at divers time. This way of Operating, Ancient Spagyrist called Detonation, a Term of Art to be learned by the Disciple of Art, as being not Common to every Rustick, in his Artifice and Experience.

This Operation being performe,d grind the hard Matter, which remained in the Pot, to a fine Powder, and upon it in another Glazed Pot pour common Water warm; which when the Matter is settled again repeat the pouring on of Water several times, until all the Salnitre be extracted: Lastly, dry the remaining Matter, and with fresh Salnitre* as much as its own weight is, burn it again, and repeat the same Operation the third time.

*[POWDER OF RULAND] Basilius doth not misguide or delude you, O Lover of Chymistry, whilst he so candidly discovers most Secret Mysteries, and so sincerely and faithfull present their wonderful Effects. As by this very Operation you have an Example: For after the first Detonation with Nitre, and so soon as you shallhave separated the Salnitre from the Powder with pure Water, you have the Powder of Ruland, with which that man effected so many Medicinal wonders, whereby he got to himself so great a Name, and so much Wealth. Which, if you prepare under a certain Constitution of Heaven (as I advised, in preparing the Liver of Antimony) you will have so much the better, by how much the more Red: for the Colour is the Soul thereof, the Effect of which in Medicine, Ruland proved and commended; but he, neither exhausted its praises, nor did he persuade the Unexperienced, that so great Virtues were latent in this Medicament. This Crocus of Metals (for so it is called) is not that, which is publicly sold in Shops, upon eight Grains of which they pour two ounces of Wine, and although the Sick only drink that wine, without any other Powder, it oftentimes works so forcibly, upwards and downwards, as either way, sometimes both ways, the life itself issues out. But the use of this is thus. Take eight, nine, ten, or eleven Grains of this our Authors preparing the first Time, according to the strength of the Sick, and all other Things co-indicating; pour on them three or four ounces of Wine; for it matter not much, whether you take more or less of the Wine. Set the Mixture in B.M. for the space of four or five hours, and so extract a most Red Tincture from this Crocus of Metals (which in an infusion of the Crocus of the Shops cannot be extracted) this Wine, no impregnated with the Sulphur of the Crocus, together with the more subtle part of the Powder, which in canting off comes out, I give to the Sick, and it purgeth kindly upwards and downwards without molestation. Nor doth this Medicament only expel Humours, but (as is proper to Antimonials rightly prepared) it strikes at the very Root of the Disease, and whatsoever in the Body is corrupted and declined

from its due state, that it amends and restores. What wonderful Effects, this only Tincture hath discovered to me, I forbear to mention, lest I should be compelled to bring their Credit in Question, who have experienced them. In this only believe me, whosoever thou art, that woulest use Chymical Medicaments, always be sure to take the true Tinctures of Things, in which their Volatile Sulphur is absconded; if you neglect this, you neglect your own Fame and Gain, and the Health of the Sick.

What remains after this third Operation grind to a subtle Powder, and on that pour the best Spirit of Wine; circulate the Mixture for one Month, in a Cucurbit or Circulatory diligently nine or ten times, so often pouring on fresh Spirit. This being done, dry the Powder with gentle heat, and for one whole Day keep it red hot in a Crucible, such as Goldsmiths use to melt their Metals in. Afterward resolve this Powder (in a moist Place, upon a Stone or Glass Table, or in Eggs boiled to an hardness) into a Liquor, which set in heat, again dry, and reduce to Powder. This Powder effects many egregious and wonderful Things, which cannot easily be believed by Those, who have not proved the same.*

*If you have believed, or experienced the virtues of this Powder once detonated, you will not be a Thomas in this third Detonation. Set to your hand, touch and use this, and it will perform the same, which true Diaphoretick Antimony can, but with greater Security and Efficacy.

But it operates not suddenly, it must have time to exercise its Powers, and shew its own Virtue, by the Testimony of Experience, very admirable.

[POWDER OF ANTIMONY, WHITE AND FIXED. ITS VIRTUES]
Whosoever labours with internal Imposthumes, let him take of this white fixed Powder of Antimony in the Spirit of Wine, or any other rich Wine, the fourth part of a Dram, five or six times a Day, and he will find his internal Imposthume opened, and all the Coagulated Blood to be expelled by degrees, without any peril of Life or Health. He, hwo is afflicted in his Body with the New Disease of Souldiers, if he use this Powder in the aforesaid manner, will also find this Evil consumed throughout the whole Body, and by the same expelled. Moreover, it produceth new Hairs, and renovates a man to the admiration of all men; it gives new, sound, and pure Blood, and is the Effecter of so much Good, as ever the least part of it (although Equity seems to require this) cannot by me be described or declared. [NO MAN MADE DOCTOR WITHOUT LABOUR] It is not fit that I should here manifest all things clearly, and in such manner, as any man, without Labour and Toyl, by reading my Writings, may become a perfect Doctor; no more than it is fit, that a Young Country Man* should be fed with the whitest and best baked Bread, which he hath not prepared with his own Labour, or the Corn of which himself thrashed not out.

*Valentine hath so clearly detected all Things, as no man, either before
or after him, hath done it more clearly. All that came after him seem to have
conspired, and agreed together to spread Clouds over that Light, which he
brought into the World. Hence it is, that they do not Publicly extol his Praises,
according to the high Esteem every man Privately hath of him; nor have they
translated his Books into other Tongues, although He, of all Authors, is the most
worthy, Who speaks in the Languages of all Nations, that he may be a comfort to
the Lovers of Chymistry, erring in the Labyrinths of others, and always produce a
new Offspring of Philosophers. But no man should think, that he could so clearly
speak, as every man, handling Chymistry (according to the saying) with unwashed
Hands, might presently understand him; that is, as himself saith, not possible to
be done, nor is it expedient that the Son of a vile Clown should eat of the finest
Flower, in preparing which he took no Pains; yet (as below he confesseth) our
Author hath used plain, simple and clear Words.*

[AUTHORS APOLOGY]
But I make too large a Progress in this open Field of Doctrine, in which Ancient
Hunters take their Larks, and the Young Ones presently follow them with their
Nets. For my Style (as all my Writings witness) hath a certain singular purposed
Method, like that of all Philosophers before me. If anyone think it strange, that
I here propose certain singular Processes, in which my Philosophy differs from
other, let him be answered with this, that Philosophic Speech much differs from
the Method of other mens Discourses, who nakedly and sincerely declare some
Process, without any Ambiguities or Cloudings of Enigmas. Therefore, consider
the difference, and accuse not me, as if I had deviated from Order, in my Style of
Philosophy, and of Preparations and Processes. For in a Philosophic Discourse,
it is not behooful to learn and judge of what appertains to the Theory, but the
Practice teacheth you the Instruction of Processes; therefore in them, true, simple,
clear and well grounded Words are to be used.

[BALSOM OF ANTIMONY] Also, of Antimony is made a Balsom, against
grievous Diseases very profitable; yet not Crude Antimony, but of the Regulus
thereof, whence may be made living Mercury, in the following manner.

Take of the best Hungarian Antimony, and crude *Tartar equal parts, and
of Salnitre half a part; grind them well together, and afterwards flux them in a
Wind-furnace; pour out the flowing Matter into a Cone, and there let it cool; then
you will find the Regulus, which thrice or oftner purge by Fire, with Tartar and
Nitre, and it will be bright and white, shining like Cupellate Silver, which hath
fulminated and overcome all its Lead.

*What I advised to in the Preparation of Liver of Antimony is here to be
repeated; instead of Crude Tartar take Salt of Tartar, by which the Operation will*

sooner and better proceed. Salnitre here is unprofitable. Therefore, take Antimony and Salt of Tartar, of each equal parts, melt them and make a Regulus, according to the Rule here given by Basilius. If you cast away the Glass (as all men for the most part do) you will do ill. [TINCTURE OF ANTIMONY, FROM ITS GLASS, ANOTHER] For I, of that prepare a very profitable Medicament in this manner. I grind this Glass in an hot Mortar, taking heed to contract no Humidity from the Air, which may easily be prevented, and having put it in a Phial, pour Alcohol of Wine thereon, and thence extract a most beautiful Tincture, in Colour red like Blood. This Tincture is a most excellent Cordial, if thirty, forty, or fifty Drops of it be taken in convenient Liquor, and that, if you will, twice or thrice a day; for it is taken with safety, and recreates the whole Man.

Grind this Regulus to a subtle Powder, and having put it into a Glass, pour it on Oil of Juniper, or Spirit of Turpentine, which comes forth in the first Distillation, and is pure as Fountain Water; keep the Vessel well closed, in a subtle heat of B.M. and the Oil of Juniper, or Spirit of Turpentine, will become red as Blood, which pour off, and rectify with Spirit of Wine. [BALSOM OF ANTIMONY, ITS VIRTUES] This is endued with the same Virtues, as Balsom of Sulphur, as I shall then show, when I write of Sulphur, because they require one and the same Preparation.

Of this Balsom only three or four Drops, taken thrice in a Week with hot Wine, heal the Diseases of the Lungs, cure the frequent Cough, and Asthma, also they are conducent in the Vertigo, prickings of the Sides and in diuturnal Coughs.

[OIL OF ANTIMONY PER SE] Also many Oils may be prepared of Antimony, some per se and without Addition, and many others by Addition. Yet they are not endued with the same Virtues, but each enjoys its own, according to the Diversity of its Preparation. Of which I now give you this Similitude. There are many kinds of Animals, which live only in the Earth, as are many Creeping Things, Worms and Serpents; also others, some of which are new kinds, which before were not, and also these proceed from Putrefaction of the Earth. Some inhabit the Waters, as all kinds of Fishes; others fly through the Air, as every Kind of Flying Things, and Birds; some also are nourished in the Fire, as the Salamander. And besides these, in the more hot Regions and Islands, are found many other Animals, which to these Nations are unknown, which prolong their Life by the Solar Heat, and which die so soon as brought into another Air. So Antimony, when prepared by the Addition of Water, assumes another nature and Complexion for operating, then when prepared by Fire only. And although every Preparation of it ought to be made by Fire, without which the Virtue of it cannot be amnifested: yet consider, that the Addition of Earth gives it wholly another Nature, than the Addition of Water. So also when Antimony is sublimed in Fire through the Air, and further prepared, another Virtue, other Powers, and another Operation follow, than in the

Preparations already described. Therefore the Oil of Antimony, per se, without addition, and the true Sulphur thereof are prepared after this Method.

[TRUE SULPHUR OF ANTIMONY]

Take crude Hungarian Antimony, put that ground to a subtle Powder, into a Glass Cucurbit with a flat bottom: pour thereon the true Vinegar of Philosophers rendred more acid with its own Salt. Then set the Cucurbit firmly closed in Horse-dung, or B.M. to putrefy the Matter for forty Days, in which time the body resolves itself, and the Vinegar contracts a Colour red as Blood. Pour off the Vinegar, and pour on fresh, and do this so often, as until the Vinegar can no more be tinged. This being done, filter all the Vinegar through Paper, and again set it, put into a clearn Glass firmly closed in Horse-dung, or B.M. as before, that it may putrefy for forty Days; in which time the Body again resolves itself, and the Matter in the Glass becomes as black as Calcanthum, or Shoomakers Ink. When you have this Sign, then true Solution is made, by which the further Separation of Elements is procured. Put this black matter into another Cucurbit, to which apply an Alembick, and distil off the Vinegar with Moderate Fire; then the Vinegar passeth out clear, and in the bottom a sordid matter remains; grind that to a subtle Powder, and edulcorate it with distilled Rain Water, then dry it with gentle heat, and put it in a Circulatory with a long Neck (the Circulatory must have three Cavities or Bellies, as if three Globes were set one above another, yet distinct or apart each from other, as Sublimatories, with their Aludel [or Head] are wont to be made, and it must have a long Neck like a Phial, (or Bolthead) and pour on it Spirit of Wine highly rectified, til it riseth three Fingers above the Matter, and having well closed the Vessel, set it in a moderate Heat for two Months. Then follows another new Extraction, and the Spirit of Wine becomes transparently red as a Ruby, or as was the first Extraction of the Vinegar, yea more fair. Pour off the Spirit of wine thus tinged, filter it through Paper, and put it into a Cucurbit (the black Matter which remains set aside, and separate from this Work; for it is not profitable therein) to which apply an Head and Receiver, and having firmly closed all Junctures, begin to distil in Ashes with moderate Fire: [GOLDEN COLOUR FROM ANTIMONY] then the Spirit of wine carries over the Tincture of Antimony with it self, the Elements separate themselves each from other, and the Alembeck and Recipient seem to resemble the form of pure Gold transparent in Aspect. In the end some few Feces remain, and the Golden Colour in the Glass altogether fails. The red Matter, which in distilling passed over into the Receiver, put into a Circulatory for ten Days, and as many Nights. By that Circulation Separation is made; for the Oil thereby acquires Gravity, and separates itself to the bottom from the Spirit of Wine; and the Spirit of Wine is again Clear, as it was at first, and swims upon the Oil. Which admirable Separation is like a Miracle in Nature: Separate this Oil* from the Spirit of Wine by a Separatory.

Here you have not only whatsoever can be made of Antimony, but also almost all that can be promised by a Chymist. This is that with which all the Books of all Chymists are filled, which is involved in so many fables, complicated in so many Riddles, and explicate with so many obscure Commentaries, that is, which in all the World is desired by Fools, sought by the Sons of Art, and found by the Wise. This Basilius reveals, this he repeats, this he inculcates; this is his Triumphant Chariot, which he as it were carries about, and often shows in the various Parts of his Writings. Before in this Treatise, he presents it under the Name of an Extraction of Crude Antimony, here it is Oil of Antimony, soon after it is converted into a Stone, which is called the Stone of Fire. Thus this Proteus often offers itself, always various, yet always the same in Substance. Compare all these Processes, which are so often diversely propounded, which these my Commentaries made upon the Extraction of Crude Antimony, and you will have the Work complete in all its Numbers; you will have a Treasure, in which, if you know not what you have, I remit you to Aesop's Dunghil-Cock, who found a Gem in the Dunghil, but knew not what he had. Consider diligently, O Lover of Chymistry, and you will find that no man hath dealt more clearly and sincerely with Thee, than Basilius, and me after him, who show thee there the Hare lies, which so many Others have hunted in vain. If now you be not here wise, you will not be healed with three Anticrya's. Therefore I will add nothing, lest I make Fools mad, who now indeed are wise.

This Oil is of a singular and incredible Sweetness, with which no other thing may be compared, it is grateful in the Use, and all Corrosiveness is separated from it. No man can by Cogitation judge, by Understanding comprehend, what incredible Effects, potent Powers, and profitable Virtues are in this Royal Oil. Therefore this this Sulphur of Antimony, I have given no other Name, than my Balsom of Life; because it effects very much, by the Grace of GOD, in those, in whom was no help to be hoped for, but by the mercy of GOD, and nothing remained by a most certain expectation of changing Life with Death; as my Brethren can witness hath been often done. It refresheth a man so, as if he were new born; it purifies the Blood; mixt and exhibited with the Tincture of Corals, it cleanseth Leprosy, and expels every Scab, which through impurity of the Blood takes Root in man. It drives away Melancholy and sadness of Heart, it confirms the Junctures, and above all strengthens the Heart, when given with the Magistery of Pearls. Also it helps the Memory, and in Swouning a more noble Medicine is not found, if six drops of it mixt with equal parts of Oil of Cinnamon be put upon the Tongue, and the Nostrils and Arteries be anointed with a little of the Essence of Saffron.

Ah Good GOD, what moves me to speak, write, and invent many Things! For I suppose I shall find few among the Doctors, who will give absolute Credit to these my Writings, which I have declared faithfully, instead of a Testament, to my Disciples, Apostles, and Followers; but Others, who before knew these wonderful

Effects, and have often in Truth experienced these Virtues, will more accurately attend, and more easily believe, and for this bounty of mine (viz. because I have opened, by the permission of GOD, the Powers and Virtues which are infused in the Creatures, and have as it were freed them from Prison, brought them to Light, and unto free Operation) give me thanks, and speak honourably of me, after I am reduced to Dust in the Grave.

[ANOTHER TINCTURE OF ANTIMONY]

Another way to drive Antimony, without Addition, over by Alembeck is this.

Make a Regulus of Antimony, by Tartar and Salnitre, as I have above taught, grind this subtily, put it in a great round Glass, and place it in a moderate heat of Sand. This way the Antimony will be sublimed: whatsoever shall be sublimed, that dayly put down with a Feather, that at length it may remain in the Bottom, and there persist until nothing more of it can be sublimed, but the whole remains fixed in the Bottom. Then is your Regulus fixed, and precipitated per se. But consider, here is required a sufficient time, and repitition of the Labour often, before you can obtain that. This Red Precipitate take out, grind it to a subtle Powder, which spred upon a flat and clean Stone, set in a cold moist Place and there let it remain for six Months; at length the Precipitate begins to resolve it self into a red and pure Liquor, and the Feces or Earth is separated from it. [TRUE SALT OF ANTIMONY] The Salt of Antimony, I say, only resolves itself into Liquor, which filter, and put into a Cucurbit, that it may be condensed by extraction of the phlegm; and again set it in moist Place, then will yield you fair Crystals. Separate these from their Phlegm, and they will be pellucid, mixt with a red Colour; but when again purified become white. Then is made the true Salt* of Antimony, as I have often prepared it.

Like with like, is a Proverb among the Greeks, and is here manifest in our Chymical Work. For this Salt acuates all Menstruums, for their more easie extraction of Metals; but those Extractions most, which are made of Antimony, as of a Mineral to it of affinity and like.

[SALT OF ANTIMONY, AND ITS USE, WHEN REDUCED TO OIL OR SPIRIT]

This Salt dry, and mix with it Venetian Earth (which is called Tripel) three Parts, and in strong Fire distil it. First a white Spirit comes off, afterward a red Spirit, which also resolves itself into white. Rectify this Spirit gently and subtily in a dry or moist Balneo, and so you will have another white Oil distilled from the Salt of Antimony. This Oil, but why do I call it Oil? this Spirit, I should rather say, since the Salt is distilled in a Spiritual Manner, in Quartans and other feavers often manifests its Virtues, and is very conducent in breaking the Stone of the Bladder; it provokes Urine, and is profitable in the Gout. Outwardly applied to old corrosive Wounds, which have their Operation from Mars, it purifies them. Also this Spirit of the Salt of Antimony purifies the whole Blood, as the Salt of Gold doth. And although, in healing very many other Diseases it may be profitably applied, yet it is not so perfect, as the above described red Oil of Antimony, in which its Sulphur is deduced to the highest, purified and separated, as I said; therefore I forbear to speak more of this.

Now, since I have treated of the Sulphur and Salt of Antimony, and shewed how they may be reduced into Oil and Spirit, to be subservient to Medicine; I here treating further, purpose to speak of its Mercury also, and to manifest what Medicine lies absconded, and as it were buried in it.

[MERCURY LIVING EXTRACTED FROM ANTIMONY]
Take the Regulus of Antimony, made in such manner, as I above taught, eight Parts. Salt of Humane Urine clarified and sublimed, one Part. Sal-Armoniack one Part: and one Part of Salt of Tartar. Mix all the Salts together in a Glass, and having poured on strong Wine- Vinegar, lute it with the Luting of Sapience, and digest the Salts with the Vinegar for an entire Month in convenient Heat; afterward put all into a Cucurbit, and in Ashes distil off the Vinegar, that the Salts may remain dry. These dry Salts mix with three Parts of Venetian Earth, and by Retort distil the Mixture with strong Fire, and you will have a wonderful Spirit. This Spirit pour upon the aforesaid Regulus of Antimony reduced to a Powder, and set the whole in putrefaction for two Months. Then gently distil the Vinegar from it, and with what remains mix a fourfold weight of the filings of Steel, and with violent Fire distil by Retort: then the Spirit of Salt, which passeth out, carries over with itself the Mercury of Antimony in the Species of Fume. Wherefore in this Operation you must apply a great Recipient with a large quantity of Water in it, so doing, the Spirit of Salt will be mixed with the Water, but the Mercury collected in the Bottom of the Glass into true living Mercury.*

*What were Arcanum's in the times of Basilius, are now in our times but vulgar Chymical Works. How often shall we find any One, who numbers himself among true Chymists, that is ignorant of the way of making Mercury of Antimony? either in this manner, as Basilius teacheth, or in another. For various Artificers have now invented various Methods, and every One useth that, he best approves of.

Behold, O Lover of Art, I have showed you, how of Antimony may be made running Mercury, which very many have so long, and in so many Parts of the World sought; and how we may use this Mercury with praise in Medicine, I will here discover and set down in Writing.

[MERCURY OF ANTIMONY, ITS MEDICINAL PREPARATION AND USE]
Take in the Name of the Lord, of this Mercury one Part, express it through a Skin,

and pour on it of red Oil of Vitriol highly rectified, four Parts. Extract the Oyl, and the Spirits of the Oyl will remain with the Mercury: Force it with vehement Fire, and somewhat will be sublimed. Thus Sublimate again put down upon the Earth in the Bottom. Then pour on other Oil, of the same weight as before, and repeat this labour a third time. The fourth time, put the Sublimate which ascends with the Earth, and grind both together, and the whole will be clear and pure, like a Speculum or Crystal. Put this into a Circulatory, and pour on it a like weight of Oil of Vitriol, and thrice so much Spirit of Wine. Circulate until Separation be made, and at length the Mercury resolve itself into Oyl, and float about like Oil Olive. When you see this, separate this Oil from the other Liquor, and put it into a Circulatory, and there pour on strong distilled Vinegar, and permit it so to rest foro about twenty Days. Then this Oil again acquires its own Gravity, and settles to the Bottom; and whatsoever Veneosity was in it, remains in the Vinegar, which will be tenebrous and altogether confused.*

There is no need of Torches at Noon Day, nor or of Commentaries in so perspicuous a Description, by which Basilius teacheth to make the Mercury of Antimony. Begin leisurely, give heed to all particulars, and your Work shall never deceive you. Lest I should darken the Author, I desist from Commenting; but add, that I doubt not, but that this Mercury will manifest wonderful Effects in the Humane Body: Yet I have not experienced its Virtues for the health of Animals, therefore my Commentaries must not exceed my Experience.

But in the Emendation of Metals, it shows itself to be endued with singular Virtues. For I say, and clearly affirm, he that can bring this Oil here described by Basilius, to the state of a fixed Stone, may glory that he aht a fixed Tincture, only inferior to the one only King of Kings, the Great Stone of Philosophers. When thou hast proceeded thus far, O Lover of Chymistry, go not back, nor take off thy hand from the Plough: but go on chearfully, perhaps in so great a Grove.

The Golden Branch, with Leaves and Twigs of Gold
Will shew itself to Thee.

[OIL OF THE MERCURY OF ANTIMONY]
This is a great Arcanum, and seems repugnant to Nature, that this Oil should first swim, and afterward being rendered more ponderous, settle to the Bottom. But consider, the Oil of Vitriol is also heavy, yet when the Mercury in its Separation is not altogether pure, it stands above it; but when the impure Lightness is taken from it by Vinegar, because the Vinegar assumes that, then the Oyl receives its just weight, becomes compact, and settles to the Bottom. This is the Oyl of the Mercury of Antimony, which is the fourth Column of Medicine.

Now come hither you Lepers! where be you? I will supply you with means for Health. This Oil is profitable against the Apoplexy, comforts the Brain, makes a man industrious, and cherisheth the vital Spirits of the Ehad. If anyone hath laboured long with grievous Diseases, and will for some time dayly use this Oil, his Hairs and Nayls will fall off, and he will be renovated, as a man newborn. All the Blood in the Humane Body is by it so purified, as every Evil is taken off from it, and expelled. This heals the French Disease, which we have lately inherited; for by this Medicine it is radically extirpated. And, to comrpehend much in few words, the praise of this Oil is greater in Medicine, than can be expressed in Speech or Writing.

Why do we, miserable Mortals, taken from the Earth, and ready to return into Earth, stick here? Why do we not hasten to give Thanks to God our Creator, for this Medicine so mercifully granted to Us? You Doctors (if it please the Gods) of either Medicine, come to me a religious man and Servant of GOD, I will manifest to you what your Eyes never saw, and will show you the way of Health and Sanity, which before you never knew. Yet if any one be found among you, who understands my Processes, and the way of Preparation, better than I; let him, I pray, not be silent, or set a Seal to his Lips: for here I stand ready to learn, nor am I ashamed further to inquire, and desire that Light, which before I knew not. For I have often said, that this our Life is circumscribed with more strait Limits, then that one man should be able to search out all Things, which Nature bears absconded in her Bosom. [IDLENESS, CONDEMNED] But on the contrary, I being the Author, let them be silent, who have experienced less than the Author, let them be silent, who have experienced less than I, and if they have not attained to a solid Understanding of my Writings, let them not attempt to amend them, or (like Brawlers) with inconsiderate Words reprehend, what they never learned in the Schools, and the Processes of which they never received from men skilled in the Law. For my Terms otherwise sound, and signify other than theirs, who oppose themselves against me, and who are shamed of the Labour of Planting Trees, and of Grafting fruitful Sprouts thereon; therefore they always abide among dry and withered Wild Trees, and can never attain to any Branch of green, sappy, and well manured Fruit Trees.

[FISHES DIE NOT OF COLD]
Hasten not, I say, O man experienced in our Art, to pass your Sentence of Judging, and be not willing to condemn, what you have not yet yourself acquired by Thoughts, or gained by Discipline. Many imprudent men frequently say, Fishes are frozen in Waters; but these discover their own imprudence and want of Knowledge. for it will never be proved, that a Fish, even in the bitterest Winter will ever be frozen in Waters, as long as the Ice of those Waters is dayly broken by the diligence of Mortals. [WHY THEY DIE IN FROZEN WATERS] But the reason why Fishes die, is because, when the Ice is not opened, their respiration is hindred, and they thence are suffocated. For it may easily be proved, that no Animal can live, when to it the Use of air is denied. Whence it may well be concluded, that those Fishes,

which are found dead under the Water, in an extreme Cold Season, die not of Cold (as men of little understanding think) but because they are deprived of Air. By like Reason (that we may apply this Example) I say; since Antimony, is to produce such admirable Fruits, it is to be taken out of the Mountains; but first, by the Care of the Miners spiracles, or breathing places, are to made for it, and afterward it must be prepared with Water, Air and Fire, as with auxiliary Mediums, lest its fruitlessness be suffocated in the Earth. But with many and laborious Preparations of Artifice, it must be manifested and brought to Light, for the expected Sanation of Diseases, by reason of which it hath been so long sought into.

[ADVICE AFTER REPREHENSION] Where now, O wretch! who contemnest Antimony, and among all men accusest it as mere Venom, where is thy Rhetorick, or Dialect, wherewith to defend thyself? But since thou understandest neither White, nor Black, nor Green, nor Red, nor Yellow; nor knowest which way to go about to justify Antimony, its Virtue, Power and Utility, being unknown to thee, thou doest well, if thou keepest Silence, and permittest this Reprehension of thy Ignorance, as a Wave driven with vehement wind to fly over thy Head; fearing, that if those Winds and Waves should be predominant, thy own weak and frail Bark would be sunk and submerged. To avoid this peril, seasonably call upon thy Sleeping Master, as the Disciples of our Saviour Jesus Christ did, when they feared they should perish. Yet this must not be done with a dissembled and feigned, but with a true and pure Heart, without all Hypocrisy; then your Redemption and Help will undoubtedly follow, so that in all Verity you will see and find the Winds and the Sea to obey you, and all Things be brought to the desired End.

I wish man were but so disposed, as he would study to obtain somewhat with labour and Diligence, then certainly the gods, the Presidents of Prosperity and Art would give Success, by which such a Disciple and Follower of Art might be assured, that in the wished School of Art, and desired Domicile of Grace, Felicity and Health hsould not be denied him, but that he himself should certainly see and find the Foundation of the Corner Stone, upon which he might commodiously build up all the other Orders of Stones. tHen would cease the so many evilly founded Impertinencies of Bablers, which in the Schools stun the Ears of Disciples, and in Houses the Ears of the Sick; and the Matter itself would speak, as it were with open Mouth, and by certain Experience confirm, that a Castle or Palace of Stone cannot so easily be set on Fire and burnt, as a Pidgeon-House, or the old Nest of a Stork composed of rotten Wood, and dayly dried more and more by the Sun.

[CENTER OF ART, NOT KNOWN BY EXTERNAL ASPECT]
But my Auditor and Disciple, do thou with sharp Judgement weigh this my sincere Information, and iwth fervent desire strive to penetrate the inmost Center of Art, which by the external Face can be known to no man; prosecute and press

after the Virtue and Power thereof, no otherwise, than as a Hunter pursues a Wild Beast; search out its Footsteps through the Snow, that you may rightly distinguish, and not take an Hart instead of an Hind, or an Hare instead of a Fox, or give a false estimate thereof, by erring from its Footsteps. Well, cast out your Nets, and take a multitude of Fishes, according to your own Wish or Desire. Place your Threads as is behooful, and dispose of the Birds, which allure others to their place, and by this way of Fowling you will fulfil your desire with profit. That by these, to every Searcher I may briefly propose my Admonition and Advice, I say: My Friend the Hunter, dispose rightly your Nets and Instruments for Hunting as behoveth; and you Mariner, who Night and Day sail through the vast Seas, and are often driven hither and thither by the Winds, give heed to the Point of your Compass, and undoubtedly you will reap profit, and not bring home your Ship, swiftly returning, without great Gain of Merchandize.

But why do I treat of many things, or spend time unprofitably (as tatling Sophisters are wont to do) in beating out the empty Chaff? I am deceived; [WORDS OF THE AUTHOR ALL OF USE] I do not unprofitably spend my time; for all the Words in my Writings are of use, and in them are found few empty Letters, which contain not some Utility together with a profitable Instruction, so that the time I spend in Writing will rather be a Recreation, than a Burthen to me. Therefore now, after the manner of Fencers, I will step back one pace, and into the Chymical Laboratory infer a new Doctrine of External Things; [ANTIMONY IS A PRESENT HELP AGAINST WOUNDS] viz. Show, that Antimony is of such a Nature, as may be prepared so, as to yield present help in Medicine pertinent to External Wounds, which manifoldly offer themselves to us, and are delcare by Chirurgy. therefore I will begin and briefly explain my Processes, viz. how that is to be used in Medicine, and how it may profitably be prepared.

Whosoever thou art, among Junior Students, that desirest to search out the Occult things of Nature, and to bring her hidden Secrets to Light, attend to what I say, that thou mayest be able to distinguish Day from Night, and what is clear from the Obscure.

[ARCANUM OF ANTIMONY]
Take of Hungarian Antimony one part, Common Salt half a part, and six parts of Argilla not burnt, grind all together, and distil vehemently with a continual Fire without Intermission and at length an Oil will come forth: from this abstract its Phlegm by Distillation, that a red dry Powder may remain in the bottom of the Cucurbit. This Powder grind subtily, and resolve it into a Liquor, upon a Marble Stone; and you will have a red shining Balsom for Wounds, which far excels very many other Balsoms. [ITS USE AND VIRTUES] Its Use* is principally in Wounds, which have been a long time open, and in the Cure of which the Doctors with their Plaisters, Unguents, Oils and Ligaments could effect nothing: but with very great Disgrace they at length take off the Horse's Bridle and Saddle, and return him to the Stable, whence they had him.

A wise General of an Army so disposeth his Soldiers in time of Fighting, that in the beginning of the Battle, the good and strong Soldiers fight, and in the End of the same the best and most strong come to deal with the Enemy; but such as are not powerful enough, for the first and last Encounter, in Arms or strength, are by him placed in the midst, that they may take Example of fighting from the Former, and hope of help and Victory from the Later. The Emperor is imitated by the Orator, in placing his Arguments so, as he may overcome the minds of men. Basilius imitates the Orator, in disposing his Processes so, as he may lead his Disciples to Sapience, and the Fruit of Wisdom. We have already had famous Processes, and in explaining them have used our Endeavour, and contributed some Light. Now follow those, that are in themselves clear enough, and not of so great moment as the former; therefore we shall not insist upon them.

[WHY THE AUTHOR SPEAKS SIMPLY]

My Form of Speaking Savours of Simplicity; for I am a man Religious, to whom the Method of Secular Men is unknown; therefore cannot so clearly detect and describe all Things, as the Matter itself seems to require. Such a man as I, as to the Terms, because he cannot so formally use them, desires to be pardoned in this, and if he neglect anything therein, he craves the candid Acceptation of all men, and in respect of his State offers himself willing and ready to serve all Christians Day and Night, and by his Prayers to GOD, to recompence this their Benevolence.

[BALSOM FOR WOUNDS, ITS USE]

This Oil is salutary in many grievous Accidents, and especially in old wounds, so that few Medicines are found, which must not give place to this. Only that Oil, which is prepared with the Vulgar Sublimate of Apothecaries, is equal unto it in Effects, and is oftentimes by Experience found to be better, especially in the Wolf and Cancer, and in the Noli me tangere. But in ordinary Fistula's, and the Herpes the superior Oyl effects wonders, which were they not confirmed by Experience, could not be believed, and all which I recite not, lest someone or other should judge me to do it from Ambition, or that thence I hunt after Fame, which was never by me either sought or desired; nor at this time, as I can holily affirm, is it aimed at by me.

[ANOTHER OIL OF ANTIMONY]

Now I will give you the Preparation of another Oil.

Take Mercury mortified (which is sublimed to clearness and Splendor, and sold by Apothecaries) and Antimony, of each equal parts. Grind them together, and distil them by such a Retort, as will retain the Spirits thrice, and afterward rectify this Oil with Spirit of Wine. Then the Operation is absolved, and the Oil becomes red as Blood; but at first it is White, and like Ice or congealed Butter. This Oil effects wonders in many Affects, where Nature gave no hope of Amendment, and it always mostly shows its force, virtue, power, and efficacy, in the perfect Emendation of Evil into Good.

By Addition may be prepared another Oil very profitable in external Wounds.

Take of Antimony one part, Sulphur one part, Sal-Armoniack, or Salt of Urine purified half a part, and Calx-vive two parts. Expel the Oil strongly: whatsoever is sublimted, that grind with the Caput-Mortuum, and thereon again pour the Oil distilled off, and thrice distil it; then the Oil is prepared. When old Wounds can in no wise be healed, then use this Oil. For it is strong, potent and penetrative: and lays a good Ground (even as Oil of Vitriol doth) for future Sanation.

[BALSOM OF ANTIMONY, AND OTHER INGREDIENTS]

An admirable Balsom of divers Ingredients (among which is Antimony) very useful in old Wounds is thus prepared.

Take of Sulphur, four ounces, set it over a moderate Fire to melt, and put into it half a pound of Mercury, and stir the Mixture so long together, as until both become one Mass. [CINNABAR, HOW MADE] This Mass grind to Powder (for it is made as Cinnabar is wont to be prepared) then grind with it four ounces of Antimony, of red Arsenick four ounces, of Crocus Martis two ounces and of Powder of Tiles eight ounces. Put all these into a Glass Cucurbit, and sublime them, as such things are wont to be sublimed; [RUBIES OF ANTIMONY] and in this Sublimation you will have Rubies in Colour not inferiour to the Oriental, but tehy are not fixed; for they are volatile, and fly from the Fire. Let the Artificer separate these Rubies from the Cinnabar, which ascends in the Sublimation, grind them to Powder and extract them with strong Vinegar. This being done, let him abstract the Vinegar leisurely in B.M. and a Powder will remain; this Powder grind small as before, and having put it into another glass, extract its Tincture with Spirit of Wine, and separate the remaining Feces. This Extraction with Spirit of Wine digest in B.M. well closed for one Month. Then abstract the Spirit of Wine, as you abstracted the Vinegar, and put the remaining Powder into a flat Glass Dish, and set that dish in a Cellar into a Pail full of Water, that it may Swim upon the Water, as a Boat. So doing, the Powder which is in the Glass will in a few days resolve it self into a clear nad perlucid Liquor.

This Liquor is salutary in old open Wounds, and is a vulnerary Balsom in like Accidents, if put into them, and they covered round with a common Stiptick Plaister. In diuturnal open Wounds, it leaves no man destitute of help, although such, as in the Cure of which all otehr Remedies have been tried in vain. Of open Ulcers, which have their Original from within, I speak not here; for they cannot perfectly be healed without internal Remedies, [ROOTS OF DISEASES MINDED BY FEW] which dry up all Fluxions, and radically extirpate the Disease: although at this time few are found, who bend their thoughts this way, or take any Course to touch the Root itself of those Diseases, of which I now treat.

If Men would in their Minds well consider the Calamities of Life, into which the Fall of our first Parents precipited us, and seriously weigh that Original Sin, and the great troop of Evills thence issuing, viz: of Sadness, Anguish, Diseases and Miseries, they certainly would spend their time better, and employ more labour to search out the health of their neighbours, so strictly commended to them by the Supreme Ruler of Heaven, and by him commanded as their proper Duty. [SUCH AS SHUN LABOUR DO NOT WHAT THEY OUGHT] But how many (with grief be it spoken!) shunning labour, consume their time unprofitably, and do not what was to be done by them, but what they formerly have done, and still ahve a lust to do, being afraid to do so much, as will soil their Fingers Ends; as if they did envy the Tradesman, who perhaps gets a small Gain by selling Soap, which they would not willingly buy, to wash their delicate hands. Are not all we miserable Mortals, that live here, Strangers in the Earth, possessing nothing, that we can call ours? [GOODS OF GOD LENT, ONLY FOR TIME OF LIFE] Are not all Things we here use, the Goods of our Lord, lent to us, whilst we live and no longer? Therefore we ought so to behave our selves in using them, taht supported with a good Conscience we may be able to stand in that Day, in which an Account is to be given for them; and be not for our Ingratitude cast into Prison, and utter Darkness where shall be weeping and gnashing Teeth. If this were the Meditation, and this the Intention of every Man, he would be like a Monster, if he should think of admitting Sin in himself, or of neglecting his Office; and all Men would, with a certain Emulation strive to pleasure their Neighbours, with the Gifts received from GOD. But these things are remote from the thoughts of the World, and Wordly Men; Money, Money, is the Scope of all their Intentions; this the Potent seek directly or indirectly, and for this the Poor are subservient to them, that they also may participate of the Mamon of Iniquity.

Yet take heed, I advise you to take heed, lest the Bones of that Flesh, sticking in your Throat, suffocate you, or the Back-bones of Fishes pierce your Heart. But what doth Admonition help which the World little esteemes of and derides? Hear, I pray you an History; or learn a Parable. [AUTHORS PILGRIMAGE] When I, according to my vow, undertook a Pilgrimage to St. James, to visit that holy Place as a Stranger, I prayed to GOD, and bound myself with a Vow, that if he granted me an happy Return to my Monastery, I would render him due Praise. He granted my Request, and I daily return Thanks to him. But I thought many more would have rejoiced with me, and have given thanks to the same GOD, for the famous Reliques, which at that time I brought with me to our Monastery, (for Consolation of the Poor, and many Others) that it might procure to it self a Name, in this perishing Valley of Tears, that could not be wiped out by any Oblivion. Yet hence few were rendered either better, or more grateful to GOD, for so great a benefit; but persevered in Derision and Contempt of that, which GOD will vindicate in the last Day.

But of these enough at this time, let us proceed in our Instruction of Antimony, whence yet another Medicine may be prepared, which I myself have experience to be very salutary; and effectual in every kind of Feavers, and in the Pestilence.

[ANOTHER OIL OF ANTIMONY PER SE]
Grind Antimony subtily, put it inot a Glass Retort, and distil it with a strong fire, without any Addition, 3 or 4 times, and always with a large Receiving Vessel; at length of it is made a Red Powder, which extract with Vinegar, and circulate the Extraction with a gentle fire for ten whole Days; abstract the Vinegar by Distilling, and that which remains, by a singular* Artifice in distilling will be changed into an Oil. Let this Oil be further Circulated until all Humidity be drawn off therefrom, and it again be reduced to Powder, as it was; when the Vinegar is abstracted and separated by Distillation, then gather the Oil in a new Receiver.

This Extraction may be rendered volatile with Spirit of Wine, after the same manner, as I taught you in former Operations.

[QUARTAN, QUOTIDIAN, AND TERTIAN FEVERS CURED]
Four Grains of this Oil taken with water of Carduus Benedictus, if the Sick be well covered and Sweated, heal Quotidian, Tertian and Quartan Fevers. The same Dose is very available for expelling the Pest, either given with Spirit of Wine, or with distilled Vinegar, according as the Paroxysm of the Pest first invades, either with Heat, or with Cold. [HISTORY OF 3 OF THE AUTHORS BRETHREN CURED OF THE PLAGUE] Which is witnessed by three Brethren in our Monastery, who recovered of the Plague by this Arcanum, when they expected no other but Death, and had made their Wills. This so reconciled their Minds to this my Art, as they helped me, with greater Zeal then before, both by their Prayers and Labour, and spent the leisure time they had exempt from Religious Duties, in serving me daily; and in a short time attained to so great Experience, that by their own Industry, and the Industry of their Brethren, they gained more true Knowledge in searching out the Arcanums of Nature, then they could before obtain in a longer series of time. Therefore, for these Men, I give them thanks, even unto my very old Age, and in very deed I return them thanks, because they deserved so well of me, and of others, by their so faithful Labour; but they finished their Course of this Life before me, and entred the way of all Flesh, wherefore I recommend their Reward to the Supreme Physitian, who dwells in the highest Heavens, and there will refresh them with sufficient Joy, and make up in Heaven that Just Recompence, which here on Earth was denied them by ignorant, and ungrateful Men.

[ANOTHER OIL OF ANTIMONY PER SE]
Another Oil of Antimony for wounds, is prepared with Addition in the following manner.

[OIL OF SULPHUR PER CAMPAN. HOW MADE] Take of Antimony, Sulphur, Saltnitre, of each equal parts; Fulminate those under a Bell, as Oil of Sulphur per Campan. is made; which way of preparing hath long since been known to the Ancients. But Consider, you will have a better way, if instead of a Bell, you take an Alembeck*, and apply to it a Recipient; so you will obtain more Oil, which will indeed be of the same Colour, as that which is made of Common Sulphur, but in powers and virtues not a little more excellent, than it.

*I now, O Lover of Chymistry, Speak to you by Pictures, not in words onely that by a Compendium of Speech, you may also have this Compendium of Labour, and Charge. Behold this Instrument, and provide for yourself such an One, that you may follow Basilius, in making Oil of Sulphur per Campan. For this way one ounce will yield you as much Oil, as a Pound will make in the Common Method. From Sixteen ounces of Sulphur you may extract half an Ounce of Oyl, which others, in their way, do scarcely expect from Sixteen Pounds.

We use 3 or 4 Drops of this inwardly taken with Spirit of Wine against the Phthisick of the Lungs; but outwardly, if it first be anointed, and a Stiptick Playster applyed, against all Wounds stinking, and tending to putrefaction, and so you will find it to be the most certain Remedy of all Wounds.

[ANOTHER OIL OF ANTIMONY PER SE]
Again another Oil of Antimony against all corroding Wounds very profitable, is this way made.

Take of Antimony, one pound, Common Salt dried, one-half pound, Tiles broken; five pounds. Grind all together, and put them into a Retort, whence distil a Yellow Oil. When all the Spirits are come forth, put the Matter in another glass. and from it extract the Phlegm, and a powder will remain; which in an humid place spread upon a stone, and you will have an Humid Balsom, which is a singular Remedy in all Verminant Wounds, and in the Cancer, which hath being cheifly in the Face of a Man, and in the Breasts of a Woman. Much more might be written of this Balsom, did I not fear, that every unskillful Man, and the Rabble of Sophisters would fall foul on me, and say I speak too largely, and commit more to writing, then Experience hath taught me; and so that I boast only of Speculations, and mere Imaginations.

[ANOTHER OIL OF ANTIMONY PER SE]
Moreover, another Oil is made in this manner.

Sublime one part of Antimony, with a fourth part of Sal Armoniack, with subtile Fire. The Salt carries up the Sulphur of Antimony, red as Blood. Grind this Sublimate to a fine Powder, and if you took at first one pound of Antimony, grind with it again five ounces of Sal Armoniack, and Sublime as before. The Sublimate dissolve in a moist place. Or otherwise, take the Sublimate, and edulcorate it from the Salt added, gently dry it, and you will have Sulphur, which burns like Common Sulphur, which is sold at the Apothecaries. From this Sulphur extract its Tincture with distilled Vinegar, and when you have abstracted the Vinegar by gentle Heat of B.M. and by a subtile Operation again distilled the remaining Powder, you will have (if in this Operation you erre not) a most Excellent* Oil, grateful, Sweet, and pleasant in its use, without any Corrosiveness or peril.

*This is another Repetition of the Process, by which the Balsom of Antimony is made, as our Author calls it in this Treatise, or the Quintessence of Antimony, of which often above. Yet in the process there is this difference, that here the Sulphur is separated by the Sal Armoniack from the Antimony, and then extracted from the Vinegar; whereas in the other Process, the Sulphur is extracted by the Vinegar, whilst it is yet united with the Antimony. But these are not things of so great a Moment, as to frustrate the Effect of Operations. Therefore this Variety gives the greater Liberty to the Operator, that he may not be Scrupulous is these Things, in which he understands the Reason of what he doth, and of the Method by which he acts.

It heals the Phthisick, remedies the Prickings of the Sides; and if any One labours with difficulty of Breathing, let him take two Grains in the morning, and as many at Night going to Bed. In the Elixir or Spirit of Wine, and he shall be healed, For it dilates the Passages of the Breast, expells all Impurities, and Phlegmes out of the Breast; and to me it hath often produced many unlooked for Effects. But cince in other Preparations of Antimony, I have described such Virtues, as with this are common to them, I Judge it needless to repeat them all, lest in the Sectators of Art I should create tediousness through multiciplity of Words, or alien thoughts by an impertinent Tautology.

In the mean while, the Liquor, which, as I above said, was resolved in an Humid Place, is an external Medicine, and very profitable; for it cleanseth the Impurities of the Skin, and if a little Oil of Tartar be mixed therewith, it heals the Phagedena of the Fingers; and it often anointed therewith, it purifies the Skin and cures Scrophulaes.

[TRUE SULPHUR OF ANTIMONY, OTHERWISE PREPARED]
Also, Sulphur of Antimony is prepared in another Manner.

Grind Antimony to a fine Powder, which boil for two hours or a little longer, in a sharp Lixivium made of the ashes of Beechwood. When boiled, filter the Antimony clear, and pour Vinegar upon the filtered Liquor, and then the Sulphur will settle to the bottom wholly red. Pour off the Phlegm and gently dry the Powder. Distil this Powder with Vinegar of Wine; extract the Tincture, and do as you did with the former Sulphur. To reduce the same into an Oil by Distilling, is worth your while: Although the Oil above mentioned hath greater Virtues, because its Body, by the Sal Armoniack, in the beginning of the Sublimation was better dissolved and opened.

There yet remain many things to be written of Antimony, and especially Three, necessary to be known by the Spagyrick Physician and Philosopher, viz. the Preparation of Vinegar, which is made of its Minera; and then the Philosophick Signate Star, which is not to be omitted; and lastly the Lead of Philosophers, of which we shall speak somewhat; touching which Many have imagined Great Things, and though (in their way of Reasoning, and Speculation) to prepare the true and sincere Mercury of Philosophers of it; which indeed cannot be done, since so great Efficacy is not from above insited in Antimony, as that in it can exist that Mercury, or of it be prepared. That Mercury is the first Ens, or first Water of Metals, which is perfect, otherwise the Great Stone of the ancient Wise Men could not be made of it. That first Ens, I say, and the Seeds thereof, are found in another Mineral, in which the Operation (according to the Genius Metals) is Particular, and most profitable Operation; and besides in it you may find whatsoever appertains to internal and external Medicine. For it is the Column of every Shop of Apothecaries, if duely prepared, as I often admonish; nor is anything wanting in it, provided the Artist hath learned well to distinguish the Disposition of Metals and Minerals, and diligently observes both the Preparation and Use of Antimony; because then, and not before, follows a perfect Judgement of it. Therefore I will stand to my Promise and comfort my Disciples, according to their Wish, by satisfying and instructing them, which way the Separation of Good from Evil may be known to them, and giving Information touching the Vinegar of Philosophers, which is made of Antimony.

[VINEGAR OF ANTIMONY]

Melt the Minera of Antimony, and purify it, grind it to a Subtile Powder, this Matter put into a Round Glass, which is called a Phial, having a long Neck, pour upon it distilled Water, that the Vessel may be half full. Then having well closed the Vessel, set it to putrefy in Horse-dung, until the Mineral begins to wax hot, and cast out a Froath to the Superficies: then 'tis time to take it out; for that is a Sign the Body is opened. This digested Matter put into Cucurbit, which well close, and extract the Water, which will have an acid Taste. When all the Water is come off, intend the Fire, and a Sublimate will ascend; this again grind with the Feces, and again pour on the same Water, and a second time abstract it, then it will be more Sharp. This Operation must be repeated, until the Water be made as Acid, as any other Sharp distilled Vinegar of Wine. But the Sublimate, the oftner the Operation is repeated, the more it is diminished. When you have obtained this Acid Vinegar, take fresh Minera as before and pour this Vinegar on it, so as it may stand above it three Fingers; put it into a Pelican, and digest it two days in Heat, then the Vinegar becomes red, and much more sharp then before. Cant this clean off, and distil it without Addition in B.M. The Vinegar comes off white, and the Redness remains in the bottom, which extract with Spirit of Wine is an excellent Medicine. Again rectify the Vinegar in B.M. that it may be freed from its Phlegm; lastly dissolve in its proper Salt, viz: in four ounces of it, one ounce of the Salt, and force it strongly by Ashes; then the *Vinegar becomes more sharp, and acquires greater Strength, and virtue.

*This Vinegar also is numbered among the chief of those things, which are prepared of Antimony, therefore I thought it worthwhile to illustrate this with some Commentaries. For although it may be made in the way Basilius prescribes, yet there are still some things wanting to render the Work both more easy and more perfect, which I here subjoin; For six pounds of Antimony are required sixteen pounds of Distilled Water, and when (after Digestion) we would distil it, a certain manual Operation must be observed, on which depends the Success of the whole Work almost. For the Alembeck must be so placed, as his Pipe or Beak may be covered with Water, which either must be put into the Recipient, or pass out by distilling into the same; otherwise the Spirit's of the Antimony will be lost, and more then half part of the same perish, or the Work require much more time for its perfection. I have expressed this by a Figure here placed, that if any by hearing do not sufficiently perceieve this, they may be seeing understand. When the whole Water hath passed over by Alembeck, the Fire (as the Author admonisheth) is to be increased, and three Days, and as many Nights continued without intermission. Then let all cool, and the Sublimate, as he teaches, must again be mixed with the Antimony; this Labour for three Days and Nights must be re-assumed, and afterwards repeated to the third time. [AUTHOR BALSOM OF LIFE, WHAT.] Then your Water will be acid, as common Vinegar. If you tinge this Vinegar with new Minera of Antimony, you will have a Tincture, which Basilius names his Balsome of Life, so often described, but never sufficiently commended. O, did Mortals know what Mysteries lie absconded in this Tincture, I question whether they would be desirous to set about any other Preparation of Antimony. All things are in this One. I have spoken, O Lover of Chymistry, do thou act.

[VINEGAR OF ANTIMONY, ITS PROPERTY]

This Vinegar Cools vehemently, not as common Vinegar, but with great Admiration, and certain Experience, especially for assuaging the Gangreane, produced from Gunpowder; also it heals other enraged Wounds and Members, when joined with the Soul of Saturn, wrought up into an Unguent, and applied outwardly. And mixt with Water of Endive, to which Salt prunella is added, it consumes the Squinancy, and extinguisheth its great Heat: besides, it assuageth the Motion of the Blood inflamed. In time of the Pestilence, taken inwardly, the Dose of one Spoonful, several times, and outwardly applied to the Swellings by

Linen Clothes moistened therein, extracts the Venom, and most excellently cools: but consider, when you would use it in this manner outwardly, it must be mixed with a third part of Water distilled from Frogspawn.

Many highly esteem the Signate Star of Antimony, and very many have endeavoured to prepare it, sparing no labour to attain the same. Which some have acquired with good success, others have lost all their labour and Cost, Many have assumed an Opinion, that this Star is the true Matter, whence the Stone of Philosophers may be made, induced hereunto, by this thought or Imagination, viz. because Nature herself hath signed it into a Star, therefore they could not choose but esteem of it, and by these Cogitations were led into the Way of Error, But I sincerely denounce, that it is nothing so. For these kind of Searchers erre from the Kings high-way, and kill themselves in clambering up Rocks and Cliffs, in which wild Goats inhabit, and Birds of Prey build their nests. It is not given to this Star to contain in itself so great Potency, or from itself to form so precious a Stone. Yet I affirm, that in it lies absconded a famous Medicine, which may be made of it. The Star is thus made.

[SIGNATE STAR OF PHILOSOPHERS]

Take of Hungarian Antimony 3. parts. of Steel 1 part. melt these together with 4. parts of burnt Tartar, when melted pour out the whole into a cone, when cold take out the Regulus, and separate it from all impurity, and the Scoria. Grind this Regulus to Powder and weigh it, then add thereto thrice so much of burnt Tartar, and pour it out as before. Repeat this labour the third time; then the Regulus purgeth itself, and becomes pure and clear. Note, when you have rightly completed the Fusion, and have used a manual Operation, as is fit (which is of principal concern in this Work) you will obtain a fair Star* bring and shining like Cupellate Silver, no less artificially formed, then if some Painter had with Compasses diligently divided the same.

*Here it is to be noted. In the third fusion of the Regulus, the Fire must be vehemently heightened, that if any Impurity remain with the Regulus, it may by that intense heat be taken away. By this means you will have a Regulus in beauty and Whiteness comparable to Silver, but in Virtue and Price far Superior.

This Star with Sal Armoniack is reduced to red *Sublimate; for the Tincture of Mars ascends. Such a Sublimate may be resolved in a moist place into a Liquor, which discovers wonderful Virtues in Chirurgy.

*This Sublimate, before it is set in a Cellar to be there resolved, should be purged from the Sal Armoniack with distilled Water. They are few Things which I admonish, but by the ignorance of these or those, great Errors are committed, and the Work with all its Costs and Charges perisheth, or at least yeilds not sufficient to pay what the Materials cost.

[ANOTHER OIL OF ANTIMONY MADE OF REGULUS]

This Regulus, or Signate Star, melted often with the Stone Serpent, is brought to such a state, as at length it consumes itself in it, and wholy unites itself with the Serpent.* This being done, the Sectator of Art hath a Matter altogether hot and fiery in which very much of Art is latent. This prepared Matter resolves itself into an Oil; this very Oil ought to be brought over the Helm by Distillation, and then rectified, that it may be pure and clear,

Of a Snake or Serpent the Nature is such, if you slacken your hold he riseth up, if you gripe him hard he bursts, the same I fear here: Therefore the Author calls that a Serpent, which he mixeth with this Regulus. But it is the Serpent of a Stone, or a Stony-Serpent; because the Salt, as a Snake willing licks a Stone.

This Oil may commodiously and securely be taken inwardly; but with great Prudence and Caution, and not oftner then twice or thrice in a Week, and no more at one time, then three Drops in two ounces of Wine, or other Water distilled from Herbs, according to the Exigency of the Disease. For this Reason, it is the Physicians part to know the Causes of Diseases, together with the Complexion of the Sick, that he may the more securely use his Remedies.

[SOME ARTS WHY SUPPRESSED]

This is a famous Acrimony* containing in itself many Arcanums; but there is no need to reveal all things together and at once to unskillful men. Some Arts are to be suppressed, that some Secrets and Arcanums may remain proper to the Philosopher, who in searching them out hath daily sustained grievous Toil.

They, who understand of how great Utility it is to extract the Essences from Metals, are not ignorant of the Virtues of this sharp Oil. For this is the only Menstruum for this purpose. How many are they who have spent their whole Life in Chymical Operations, and never could arrive to the knowledge of a true Menstruum? To thee it is here revealed, if Health be your aim, you may safely use it in the Body; if you attempt somewhat more sublime, and have already conceived good hope you shall compound it, this is the principal help of all, for ascending to the Throne of the Chymical Kingdom.

But let him, who resolves to tread in my Footsteps not be weary of Searching; but what I have done, let him do, and what I have so often desired, and what with so earnest Wishes I have sought, let him seek. These Principles, which I have prescribed you, are sufficient for to search out the End by. Many have failed, yea many have been cut off by Death, before they could in their Learning attain to the Principles only; that is, they are deprived of Life, before they could acquire the Magistery of Art. Therefore, I at first set forth a Book of Rudiments, that the

Studious follower of Art (who in his first Experiences had need of so much time) might the sooner attain his desired end, and wished Scope, and next unto GOD give me thanks.

[ANOTHER OIL OF ANTIMONY MADE OF REGULUS, ITS EFFECTS]
Moreover, in this Oil a wonderful Effect is latent. For if this Oil be circulated with Crystals for sometime, viz. for three Days and Nights (the Crystals being first Calcined) it from them extracts a Salt: which being done, the Oil may again be distilled off by Retort. Thus you will have a Medicine, which admirably breaks the Stone in the Bladder, and expels it, and there also effects many other Things, by a certain famous virtue in it.

[LEAD OF PHILOSOPHERS]
But that we may also say something of the Lead of Philosophers, let the curious searchers of Nature know, that between Antimony and common Lead, there is a certain near affinity, and they hold a strict friendship each with other. As a Tree casts out of its side it's superfluous Rosin, which is the Sulphur of that Tree; as the Cherry-tree, and other Trees, which give forth such Gums: there are other kinds of Trees also, which by reason of their abundance of Mercury, produce and cast forth from themselves a certain Excrescency, which neither in Form, nor Virtue is in any wise like to their Fruit; but hath wholy other properties, as in Oaks and Apple-trees is apparent, which produce like bastard Fruits, or Monsters: So the Earth also hath like abortive Fruits, which in Separation from the pure Metals, are severed and cast out.

Now although there is so strict an affinity between Antimony, and Saturn; yet by reason of the too much Sulphur, which Antimony hath in itself, it is cast out from it: because its viscous Body (in it's Nativity) could not come to perfection; and therefore it was constrained necessarily to consist among Minerals: because it's abundance of hot Sulphur was the Cause, that hindred it's Mercury, that through defect of Cold it could neither come to Coagulation, nor into a Malleable Body. Morever, I say, the Lead in Antimony is no other, then its Regulus, which hath not as yet obtained Mallaeableness. And, as above I said, when the Regulus and Steel by Liquefaction are united, and deduced to a Star, there are many, who would thence make the ancient stone of Philosophers; which I before denied to be possible. Yet what Medicines may be prepared of it, you have already briefly heard; therefore touching them, I shall not add a Word more.

[WHY THE REGULUS IS CALLED LEAD]
But the Reason, why the Regulus is called and accounted Lead, is this. When that Regulus is taken, which Antimony gives forth from itself in making glass, and put into a Crucible well closed, which can resist the fire, with the Salt of Saturn (having been first Cemented with the Salt for three hours) and these

permitted to melt together, in a Wind Furnace, the *Regulus, when taken out, is found to be rendered soft, and more ponderous, then it was before. For it receives it's ponderosity from the Spirit of the Salt, which also gave it softness, so that it's Body now is compact and heavy.

*I not enviously, as many Chymists do, but affectionately deal with Chirurgeons: wishing that they would in their mind, as according to their faculty they may and ought, endeavour to prepare such helps, for their miserably afflicted Patients, and such Compendiums of Sanity, as may be prepared of this Regulus. Would you have me discover to you the Mystery? Hear with pleasure, and use it. This Regulus, by the Salt of Saturn rendered Malleable, must be mixed with equal parts of Mercury condensed by Saturn, and in a vehement fire fluexed, and so well mixed. The Matter comes forth, in it's external Face like unto Silver, but in its internal Virtues is more noble, and more precious than any Silver. But you Chyrurgeon, studious of your own Art, and by Art covetous of Glory, deduce that into thin plates, and externally apply it to Wounds, and Malignant Fistula's. So doing, you will be amazed, when you shall see Nature, helped by this Art, to perform more, in a very short time, then you could have hoped for in a longer time, by so many Unguents and Plaisters. The Rusticks (to use the Words of Basilius) will no more deride and upbraid you, saying, they can effect more with a piece of crude and stinking Lard, then you are able to do with the laborious Process of your whole Chirurgick Art.

Therefore I say, there is not much difference between the Stignate Star, and Lead of Antimony; which notwithstanding are every where distinguished as two diverse things. For either of them is made of the Glass of Antimony, and prepared into one and the same Medicine, as is already by me sufficiently declared. Here therefore I break off my Discourse, that I may explain what the stone of fire is, after I shall have declared the Appendix which follows.

O GOD grant thy Grace, and open the Hearts and Ears of Men unwilling to hear, and to them impart thy Blessing, that they may acknowledge Thee in thy Omnipotency, and wonderful Works of Nature, to thy Praise, Honor and Glory, and for the Health, Solace, and Confirmation of the Strength of their Neighbour, and also for Restoring the Sick to their Pristine Health. Amen.

THE APPENDIX

For a Conclusion you are further to know, that Antimony may be applied to many other Uses, then as above expressed, as to Scripture or Printing, for which Printers use it. Also under a certain Constellation and Concourse of the Planets, a Mixture of Metals is made with Antimony, of which Artists form Signatures and Characters endued with singular Virtues. Of the same Mixture also are made Speculums, of many and wonderful Aspects and Properties. Also Bells and other Instruments may be made thereof, of admirable sound. Likewise Images of Men, and many other Things*.

[ANTIMONY ITS WONDERFUL VIRTUES, THE HUNDREDTH PART OF THEM NOT KNOWN] *The virtues and powers of Antimony which the Author here in this Appendix so lightly toucheth, and passeth over, are so many and so various, as indeed the hundredth part of them is not yet known to Men. Which Ignorance undoubtedly redounds to the Reproach and Ignominy of our kind; because we Men, among so many other Animals, only endued with Reason, and a Faculty of Discoursing, are hurryed with so great impetuousness, to that wicked and abominable Desire of Gain, as scarcely any Man hath leisure to search out the Wonders, which the Author of Nature hath insited in his Creatures. But I am unwilling to repeat this Reprehension so often spoken of by Valentine; I do only call it to mind. This Mineral, in which lies hid so admirable Spirit, that by Exhausting it cannot be exhausted, hath also Virtues, which by no man studying can be sufficiently known. What I have tried, out of the way of Chymistry and Medicine are few; yet Experience hath taught me so much, as I judge Antimony in other things will show itself no less admirable, then in Chymistry and Medicine.

Yet what I think of Characters and Signatures, which the Author saith may be made under a Concourse of certain Constellations, I shall not here discover. It sufficeth me, that I can say, that among all Metals and Minerals, there is not any Substance known, which contains so much of a Celestial Spirit, and hath so great Sympathy with the Stars, as Antimony. Weigh this, with all that I have before said of Antimony, but not negligently, and Hasten to the Stone, which is called the Stone of Fire.

But since these things concern not Medicine, nor appertain to my Order, Rule, and Calling, I rest well satisfied in my Vocation, and commend them to the Handling of Others, who know them better.

OF THE TRIUMPHANT CHARIOT OF ANTIMONY
AND
What the STONE of FIRE is.

[AUTHORS PARABLE]

When, at a certain time an abundance of Thoughts (which my internal and fervent Prayer to GOD suggested) had set me loose and wholy free from all terrene Businesses, I purposed in my self to attend to Spiritual Inspirations, of which we have need, for the more accurate scrutiny of Nature. Therefore I resolved to make myself Wings, that I might ascend on high, and inspect the stars* themselves, as Icarus, and his Father Daedalus in times past did, if credit may be given to the Ancient Writings of Poets.

*This Leave is to be given to all, who treat of Sacred Things, viz. to declare those things, which they are willing to discover (not to the unlearned ignorant Deriders, but only to Men, worthy, and to such as sincerely desire, and aspire to the knowledge of the same) in a certain singular and Parabolical kind of Writing. In which our Author is the more to be excused, because when he comes to the greatest of Mysteries, which he intended to explain in this Book, he betakes himself to certain hiding Places of Parables, and with the Heaven of Piety, which is wont to cover all things (yea even the most wicked) he so veils his Secrets, as None but Pious and sincere Disciples of Art can with the acuteness of their sight penetrate these Clouds. Do thou therefore, with a certain intellectual Luxury sport with him, he will not delude thee.

But when I soared to near the Sun, my Feathers with it's vehement heat were consumed, and burnt, I fell headlong into the depth of the Sea: yet to me, in this my extreme Necessity invoking GOD, help was sent from Heaven, which freed me from all peril and the present Destruction. For an Angel hastened to my assistance, who commanded the Waters they should be still, and instantly, in that deep Abyss appeared a most high Mountain, upon which at length I ascended, [INFLUENCE OF SUPERIORS ON INFERIORS] that I might thereon examine, whether (as Men had affirmed) there was any Friendship* and Familiarity between Superiors and Inferiors, and whether the Superior Stars have acquired power from GOD, their Creator, to produce any one Thing like themselves in the Earth.

*There hath been no Man, who had darted his sight but as it were through a Lattice, into the Penetrals of Chymistry, who did ever deny this Influence of Superiors upon Inferiors. Therefore let Basilius so holily affirming, and so often openly declaring it to Men, be credited by those, who, the true Light being not yet risen upon them, do by feelign without sight practice Chymistry.

And having searched into Things, I found, that whatsoever the Ancient Masters had so many Ages since committed to Writing, and delivered to their Disciples, who earnestly desired to be the true Imitators of them, was (as I may say) more true than Truth itself. Wherefore, as is fit, I give praise and thanks to my Lord and Heavenly Father, for his incomprehensible Works.

[MINERALS HOW MADE] In very deed (that I may expound the matter in few Words) I found all Things, which are generated in the Bowels of Mountains, to be infused from the Superior Stars, and take their beginning from them, in the form of an aqueour Cloud, Fume or Vapour, which for a very long time fed and nourished by the Stars, is at length educted to a tangible form by the Elements. Moreover, this Vapor is dried, that the Wateriness may lose its Dominion, and the Fire next, by help of the Air, retain the Ruling Power. Of Water Fire, and of Fire and Air Earth is produce: which notwithstanding are found in all things consisting of Body, before the Separation of them. Therefore this, viz. Water is the first Matter* of all things, which by the Dryness of Fire and Air is formed into Earth.

*This is an Old Song, this is the Sum of Art; from this Imitation of Nature is found the lesser Stone of Fire, from this it is made, whensoever it is prepared, from the Same also the great Philosophick Stone derives its Original. [WATER OF ANAXAGORAS, WHAT] This is the water of Anaxagoras, the Fire of Empedocles, and Aristotle's first Matter, of which all things have been, and to this Day are made. Which is clearly evident in the Nutrition of Man, the Growth of a Tree, and in the Generation of Metals, for that, which constitutes Flesh, Woods, and Metals, is not taken from Food, Rain or Earth, but is infused into them from elsewhere. [ALIMENT, WHICH NOURISHETH ALL THINGS, WHAT] That very Thing is the Aliment, which nourisheth all things, but that it may be so variously specificate, it must be separated from that Body, in which it dwells, and by joined to another, which by the Chymical Art is performed.

But now since my Intention is to describe the Stone of Fire, how it is made of Antimony, together with the Process of its Preparation, which not only heals Men, but Metals also particularly; it will be necessary before all Things, to speak somewhat of these following Heads. What properly the Stone of Fire is; what is its Minera; whether a Stone can be made without Matter or no; what is the extreme difference of Stones, and how many Species of them are found, and lastly of their use.

[AUTHORS PRAYER] In this my purpose, I pray, O spirit of Heaven illuminate me, that I may give a true and sincere Instruction, viz. according as is fit for me, and the matter itself permits. Indeed I have hopes of Eternal Absolution *from this my Supreme confessor, who from Eternity possesseth the Throne of Mercy, and will give Testimony of all things, when the Decretory Sentence shall be pronounced upon all Men, in the Last Judgement, without any appeal.*

[TRUE TINCTURE OF ANTIMONY NOT MADE OF CRUDE AND MELTED ANTIMONY]
Therefore first know and consider, that the True Tincture of Antimony, which is the Medicine of Men and Metals, is not made of crude and melted Antimony, as it is sold by Merchants and Apothecaries; but extracted from the Minera, as it is taken out of the Mountains, and before it is formed into Glass. But how that Extraction should be made, is the principal Work in which the whole Art consists: Health and Riches attend him, who rightly attains to that. [TRUE TINCTURE OF ANTIMONY NAMED THE STONE OF FIRE] But, my Reader, you must diligently mind this, viz. that the Tincture of Antimony prepared fixed and solid, or the Stone of Fire (as I name it) is a certain pure, penetrative spiritual and fiery Essence, which is reduced into a coagulated Matter, like the Salamander, which in Fire is not consumed, but purified and conserved.

Yet the Stone of Fire tingeth not universally, as the Stone* of Philosophers, which is made of the Essence of Gold itself. To this no such power is given, as that it should perform such things, but it tingeth particularly; viz, Silver into Gold, Tin also and Lead; but Mars and Venus it toucheth not, nor do they yield more, then from them by Separation may be effected.

[THE DIFFERENCE BETWEEN THE STONE OF FIRE AND THE STONE OF PHILOSOPHERS] As much as Heaven is elevated above the Earth, so much doth the true Stone of the Philosophers differ from this Stone of Fire. I myself do candidly confess, that although I have found this, yet I am very far distant from the other. And this, whatsoever it is, I own to be received from the Wisdom of Basilius. Do you take heed you be not deluded by your own Fantasy, and that others deceive you not.

Moreover, one part of it can tinge no more, then five parts of Metal, so as to persist in the Trial of Saturn and Antimony; whereas, on the contrary, the Great Stone of Philosophers can transmute to infinity. Also in augmentation it cannot be so far exalted; yet the gold is pure and solid.

[EARTH OF ANTIMONY] The Minera, out of which this Stone or Tincture is made, is no other then (as I above mentioned) the very Earth of Antimony; from which, I say, it is made: but how or with what virtue, force, and power it is endued, you shall hear anon.

[POWDERS FIXED, WHY CALLED STONES] Let the Reader consider, that there are many kinds of Stones found, which tinge particularly; but all fixed Powders, which tinge, I here signify by the name of Stones; yet one tingeth more highly then another, as especially the Stone of Philosophers, which obtains the principal place; [TINCTURES, THEIR DIFFERENCE] the next is the Tincture of Sol; and of Luna. For the White: after these, the Tincture of Vitriol or Venus; likewise the Tincture of Mars; either of which hath in it self the Tincture of Sol, when reduced to Fixation. Next to these follow the Tinctures of Jupiter and Saturn for Coagulation of Mercury; and lastly, the Tincture of Mercury itself. This is the difference and multiplicity of Stones and Tinctures, all which notwithstanding are generated from Seed, and from one original Matrix, from which the true Universal Stone proceeds, but out of these no other Metallic Tincture is to be found. But all other Things, by what name soever called, all Stones (whether precious or common) I touch not now, nor have I any Intention to write or speak anything of them at this time; because they contain in themselves no other Virtues, then what appertain to Medicine. Nor shall I here make mention of Animal or Vegetable Stones; because they are only conducent to Medicine; but for Metallic Works unprofitable and void of all Virtue. Yet all the Virtues of all Things, Mineral, Animal, and Vegetable, collected into one, are found in the Stone of the Philosophers.

[SALTS, ENDUED WITH NO TINGING VIRTUE] Salts are endued with no tinging Virtue, but are only Keys* for the Preparation of Stones; otherwise of themselves they effect nothing.

*[SALTS ARE KEYS] *Salts, as here is rightly said, are Keys; they open the Chest wherein the Treasure lies. But you must be sure to take the true Key; otherwise you may spoil the Lock, and not open the Chest. It is not safe in this Case to take Quid for Quo, as Apothecaries are wont. You must have a Philosophic Key, and proper Salts fit for opening must be taken. Nor condemn this Distinction, which is intimated, between Salts opening, which the Author here calls (as they are) Kleys, and Salts fixing, which enter the Treasure itself; as is sufficiently manifest by the Text.*

[FIXATION, WHENCE] Yet, as for Metallic Salts (I now speak to the purpose if you rightly understand, what distinction I put between Mineral Salts) they are not to be slightly esteemed, nor to be rejected in Tinctures, since we can in no wise be without them, in their Composition, For in them lyes that most precious Treasure, from which every Fixation derives its Original.

[A STONE, WHETHER MADE WITHOUT MATTER] Here some may ask, and indeed very properly; whether such a Stone can be made without matter? I answer, No. For every Thing must have its own Matter; but not without Distinction. Animals require their Matter, Vegetables theirs, and Minerals theirs. Only consider and before all things observe this; [FERMENTATION, NECESSARY, WHY] viz. that no Body can be profitable for any Stone, without Fermentation, which I find in the end of the Work (I mean as to the Preparation of the Great Stone) cannot be omitted, if I would convert Metals with gain; for although in tangible is taken; yet from that formal Body must be extracted a certain Spiritual and Celestial Entity (shall I call it) or Apparency; for I find no other more fit name to give it: which Entity was by the Stars, before infused into that Body, and by the Elements concocted and made perfect. Yet this Spiritual Entity must again by a lesser Fire, and by the Regimen and Direction of the Microcosm, be reduced to a tangible, fixed, Solid and inconsumptible Matter.

But what do I, or what do I speak? I act as if I were deprived of my Reason*, in uttering words so openly. For if I had either Reason or Judgement, I should not discover so great Things with my Tongue, or command my hand to proceed in writing them.

*Art thou well in thy Wits, Basilius, who doest thus prostitute the Arcanum of the Stone, which hath unto this day been so diligently absconded by all Philosophers? Surely, if thou hadst not laboured with I know not what Intemperance of Mind, thou wouldst have closed thy Lips, and not have so clearly opened, what it is to separate the Pure from the Impure, what to render the fixed volatile, and again to fix that; how the Inferior becomes Superior, and that again plunged into the Deep Abyss, from which it had ascended. To discover so many Mysteries, in so few Words, as here thou doest, assuredly if it be not Madness, it is a certain very great benevolence to Posterity. This is that which moved him. Valentine seems to have burned with this Affection, and could not overcome that Inclination of Well-doing to many, by the Obligation (imposed on all Philosophers) of concealing the Secret Mystery of Nature, which by the Author thereof, that is, by Nature naturating with Intellectual Revelation, is communicated only to the Sons of Art worthy and chosen. The Secret of Secrets hath fallen from Basilius, do thou Reader attend, if you find the Pearl, be not like Aesop's Cock.

All Tinctures of Metals ought to be separated, as that they may be moved with a certain principal Love and Affection to Metals, and have a propensity and desire of uniting themselves with tehm, and of reducing them to a better State. Will you have an Emblem, or Example? [EXAMPLE OF MAN AND WOMAN] Behold here it is of Man and Woman. If they two be inflamed with Mutual Love, neither Delay, nor Rest is admitted, until they be united, and their Desire satisfied: after this Union they rest, and are multiplyed, according to the good pleasure of GOD, and the promise of his Blessing.

Man lives obnoxious to many and perillous Diseases, some of which debilitate and consume the powers of Nature so, as the Man can by no Remedies be perfectly restored to Health and his former Strength [LOVE, A DISEASE] But Love is a disease, with which no other Disease may be compared, which is not healed unless by Production of its own like, which either Sex desireth, and that Desire is not satisfied, unless by fulfilling his will of the enkindled affection. How many Testimonies of this violence, which is in Love, are daily found? for it not only inflames the Younger Sort, but it so exagitates some Persons far gone in years, as through the burning Heat thereof, they are almost mad. Natural Diseases are for the most part governed by the Complexion of Man, and therefore invade some more fiercely, others more gently; but Love, without distinction of poor or rich, young or old, seizeth All, and having seized so blinds them, as forgetting all Rules of Reason, they neither see or fear any Snare. Peculiar Members are infected with the Singular Symptoms of other Diseases, all the other parts remaining sound and free from that Dolour. Whom Love infects, it invades all over, penetrates the Body and its whole Substance, Form, and Essence, and leaving nothing unoffended. For taking place in the Heart there it kindles a Fire, the burning heat of which is diffused through the Veins, Arteries, and all the Members of the body, and in a word I say, where Love once hath fixed its Root, the man is so deprived of all sense, reason and understanding, as he forgets all things, seriously minds nothing; he is unmindful of GOD and his Law, his promises and threats he little regards; the torments of Hell and rewards of Eternal Life he condemns. I speak of inordinate and unlawful Love, to which, if a man be once addicted, he adheres so pertinaciously, as nothing can reclaim, nothing can restrain him; he forgets his Duty, Calling and Condition; derides all admonition, despiseth the Counsels of Parents, Superiors, and others who wish him well; briefly I say, he is so blind with Love as he cannot see his own Misery; so deaf, as he cannot hear those, who by their faithful advice, endeavour to turn and avert from him, the damage and evil, which would befall him. Love leaves nothing entire, or sound in the Man; it impedes his Sleep, he cannot rest either Night or Day; it takes off his Appetite, that he hath no disposition either to Meat or Drink, by reason of the continual Toerments of his Heart and Mind. It deprives him of all Privdence; hence he neglects his Affairs, Vocation, and Business; he minds neither Labour, Study nor Prayer; casts away all thoughts of any Thing but the Body beloved; this is his study, this his most vain Occupation. If to Lovers the Success be not answerable to their Wish, or so soon and prosperously as they desire, how many Melancholies hence arise, with griefs and sadnesses, with which tehy pine away and wax so lean, as they have scarcely any flesh cleaving to the Bones; yea, at length tehy loose the Life itself, as may by many Examples! [LOVES SAD EFFECTS] For such Men (which is an horrible thing to think of) slight and neglect all perils and detriments, both of the Body and Life, and of the Soul and Eternal Salvation.

[AUTHORS CONTINENCY] But of these enough; for it becomes not a Religious Man to insist too long upon these Cogitations, or to give place to such a flame in his heart. Hitherto (without Boasting I speak it) I have throughout the whole course of my Life kept myself safe and free from it, and I pray and invoke GOD to vouchsafe me his Grace, that I may keep holy and inviolate the Faith, which I have Sworn, and live contented with my Spiritual Spouse, the Holy Catholic Church. [TINcTURE OF ANTIMONY OUGHT TO HAVE LOVE TO METALS] For no other reason have I alleged these, then that I might express the Love, with which all Tinctures ought to be moved toward Metals, if ever they be admitted by them into true Friendship, and by Love, which penetrates the inmost parts, be converted into a better State.

Now let us proceed to the Preparation of the Stone, and leave its use to the Close of this Discourse. This Stone is of a penetrable and fiery Nature, is cocted and brought to Maturity by fire, no otherwise, then all other Things, which are found in this Orb; which notwithstanding as they are of a diverse Nature, so they in diverse manners obtain that, according as the Nature of Things supplies with Disverse Fires.

[DIVERSE FIRES] The first Fire is Celestial, by GOD kindled in our Hearts, by which being inflamed we are moved with Love and a certain confidence in and of GOD our creator, of the Most Holy and incomprehensible Trinity, and of the Mercy, Grave of our Saviour JESUS CHRIST; which Confidence kindled is Us by Love, never fails, never deserts us in our Necessities, but will most certainly deliver our Souls from everlasting destruction. The second Fire is Elemental, produced by the Sun, and tends to the Ripening of all things in the Macrocosm. The third Fire is corporal, with which all Foods and Medicines are cocted and prepared, without which Men can neither obtain Health of Body, nor sustentation of Life. Of a fourth Fire mention is made in the Sacred Scriptures, viz. that, which before the Supreme Judgement of GOD shall consume this visible World: but what Fire is, and how it shall operate, that (if we be wise) we must leave to be judged of by his own Supreme Majesty. A fifth Fire is also spoken of in Holy-Writ, viz. Eternal Fire, in which never to have end, the Divels shall never be set at liberty from their Infernal Prison, and wicked Men, their Companions, adjudged to those Eternal Fires, shall be vexed, punished and miserably tormented forever: from which I pray the Omnipotent and merciful Lord to preserve us. Here I would admonish all and every Creature endued with Reason, by their Prayers to beg that Grace and Mercy from the Omnipotent, that they may so conform their Life to the Divine Precepts, and their own Duty, as that they may escape this Fire, and its Eternal Torments.

Our stone of Fire (which is to be noted) must be cocted ripened with Corporal Fire in the Microcosm, as all other Medicines and foods are prepared by the same. For where the great Fire of the Macrocosm ceaseth from it's Operation, there the Microcosm begins to produce a new Generation; therefore this Concoction should seem strange to no Man. [EXAMPLE OF CORN] Corn is augmented and ripened by the Elementary Fire of the Macrocosm; but by the Corporal Fire of the Microcosm a new Coction and maturation is effected, that man may use and enjoy that Divine Gift for his sustentation, and by the same perfect the Last and the Least, which is produced of the first and the Greatest.

The true Oil of Antimony, of which the said stone of Fire is made, is above measure sweet, and from it's earth is in such wise purged and separated, as if a Glass full of it be exposed to the Sun, its casts forth various and wonderful Rays (as if many fiery Speculums were there present) resembling a Ruby and other Colours. Now attent O lover of Art and Truth, and hear what I shall teach.

[ITS PREPARATION] Take in the Name of the Lord, of the Minera of Antimony, which grew after the Rising of the Sun, and Salt Nitre, of each equal Parts; grind them subtily and mix them; burn them together with a moderate Fire very artificially and warily; for in this the principal Part of the Work consists. Then you will have a matter inclining to Blackness. Of this matter make Glass, grind that Glass to a subtile Powder, and extract from it an high red Tincture with sharp distilled Vinegar, which is made of it's proper Minera. Abstract the Vinegar in B.M. and a Powder* will remain, which again extract with Spirit of Wine highly rectified, then some feces will be put down, and you will have a fair, red, sweet Extraction, which is of great Use in Medicine. This is the pure Sulphur of Antimony, which must be separated as exactly as is possible.

*Take heed, take heed, O Lover of Chymistry, lest by this Fire, you burn the Wings of your Bird, which hath now raised itself to the top of Mountains. Few words are sufficient to the Intelligent, there is no need to inculcate the same things often, our careful Father Basilius doth that often enough.

If of this Extraction you have one pound two ounces take of the Salt of Antimony, as I taught you to prepare it, four ounces and on them pour the Extraction, and circulate them, for a whole Month at least, in a Vessel well closed, and the Salt will unite itself with the Extracted Sulphur. If Feces be put down, separate them, and again abstract the Spirit of Wine by B.M. The Powder which remains urge with vehement Fire, and not without admiration will come forth a varicoloured sweet Oil, grateful, pellucid and red. Rectify this Oil again in B.M. So that a fourth part of it may be distilled, and then it is prepared.

This Operation being completed, take living *Mercury of Antimony, which I taught you how you should make, and pour

*This word, our Mercury, which hath so often rendred Thee ambiguous, is also here to be understood: for if you take not the true Mercury of Philosophers, you do nothing. Whosoever he be, that shall candidly tell you this, he will be to you Pylades, and you to him Orestes, and nothing will be more pleasant to me in Life, then to join myself to you, as a third Sociate in Friendship.

upon it red Oil of Vitriol made upon Iron, and highly rectified. By Distillation in Sand remove the Phlegm from the Mercury; then you will have a precious Precipitate, in Colour such, as never was any more grateful to the Sight; and in Chronical Diseases and open Wounds, it may profitably be used for recovering the Pristine Sanity. For it vehemently dries up all Symptomatical Humors, whence Martial-Diseases proceed; in which the Spirit of the Oil, which remains with the Mercury, and conjoins and unites itself thereto, powerfully helps.

Take this precipitate, and of the Superior Sweet Oil of Antimony, equal parts, pour these together into a Phial, which well closed set in convenient heat, and the Precipitate will in time resolve and fix itself in the Oil. Also the Phlegm by the Fire will be consumed, and what remains become a Red, dry, fixed and fluid* Powder which will not in the least give forth from itself any Fume.

*Far hence, far hence ye Prophane, and you that are initiated in the Sacred Mysteries of Chymistry keep silence. Let the King enter into his Bed-Chamber, that he may consummate his Marriage.

O tua te quantis attollet Gloria rebus,

Connubio tali!

Yet make not too much hast to enter, or disturb this Matrimonial Conjunction, let them for many Months delight themselves with their mutual Embraces, and not go forth, until from their mutual Love they be changed into an Hermaphroditic Body, and have produced that Son desired by all, if not a King of Kings, yet at least a Regulus or Ruler, which delivers his Subjects from Diseases and Necessity.

Now my Follower, and Disciple of Arcanums, I will speak after a Prophetic manner. When you have brought your Philosophic Studies (in the Method by me prescribed) to this end, you have the Medicine of Men and Metals; which is grateful and Sweet in use, without all peril, it is penetrative, yet causeth not Stools, it induceth Emendation, and expells Evil. Use it as is fit, and it will yield you many Commodities, both for health and temporal necessity; by which means you will be freed from want in this World; which is a thing of so great Moment, as no Sacrifice of Gratitude can be found sufficient to answer this favour of GOD showed to you.

Here, O my GOD, I as a Religious Man am troubled in Mind; and know not whether I do well or ill, whether in * speaking I have exceeded or not reached the due Bounds; whilst I propose, and show to everyone, as it were, his proper House. Do thou, that art a young Follower of Art, inquire, search and try, as I have done; if you attain your End, give greatest thanks to GOD, and after him to me your Master. But if you turn aside into devious and by-paths, blame yourself, not me; for I am not guilty of your Error.

Our Author judgeth himself to have spoken too much, if you also think the same, you will rejoice in his Sadness. Yet it is strange, that no Man can contribute a little Light to this Philosophy, but he presently repents.

Now I have said enough, and writ enough, and taught so clearly and openly, and plainly, as more manifestly or clearly cannot be done by Writing, unless some lost and rash Man, knowing and willingly would cast himself into Hell, to be there Submerged and Perish: Because, by the Creator of all Things we are most severely prohibited further to unlock these Mysteries, or to eat of the Tree which was planted in the midst of Paradise. Therefore here I will desist, until Others show, what is here to be done by Me, and what they judge is to be omitted, and say no more of this, but pass to its Use.

[ITS USE, DOSE, ETC]

Therefore know, that the Use consists in Observation of the Person and his Complexion, with relation to what appertains to Humane Health, that Nature be not overpowered with too great a Quantity, or not helped by too small. Yet too much is not so Religiously to be feared; for it will not readily hurt; because it helps to recover the pristine Sanity, and fights against Venom, if any be in the Body. This I only add, three or four grains of it, given in one only Dose, are sufficient for expelling every Evil, if taken in Spirit of Wine. For this Stone or Tincture passeth through all the Members of the body, and contains in itself the Virtues of many Arcanums. It remedies the Giddiness of the Head, and all Diseases, which have their Original from the Lungs. It cures difficulty of Breathing, and the Cough; the Leprosy and French Disease are amended by it, in a wonderful manner. The Pest, Jaundices, Dropsies and all kinds of Fevers, are often cured by it, Likewise it expels Venom taken. It profits those, who have drunk a Philtrum or Love-potion: it confirms all the Members, Brain, Head, and all things depending thereon. It helps the Stomach and Liver; heals all Diseases, which proceed from the Reins; cleanseth the impurity of the Blood. Also this Tincture of Antimony, breaks the Stone of the Bladder to Powder; and expells it; it provokes Urine, when stopped by Flatus's. It restores the vital Spirits, cures Suffocation of the Matrix, makes the Menstrues flow if stopped and stays them if inordinate. It causeth Fruitfulness, and makes the Seed sound, and available for Generation, both in Women and in Men. Lastly, this Stone of Fire inwardly taken (convenient Plaisters being also outwardly applied) heals the Cancer, Fistula's, Rotteness in the Bones, and all corroding Ulcers, and whatsoever takes beginning from the Impurity of the Blood, also the Disease itself called Noli me tangere. And that I may comprehend all in few Words, this Stone, like a Particular Tincture, is a * Remedy against all Symptoms, which can happen to the Humane Body. All which Experience will very clearly demonstrate to you, and open the way further to you, if you be a Physician, called by GOD to that Office.

Here the Medicinal Virtues are spoken of at large. For Basilius supposeth Thee not to be defiled with the Filths of Avarice, but splendid in the Light of Charity, and burning with a Desire of helping thy Neighbour, following him discovering thse Secrets. Now farewell, O Lover of Chymistry, and if thou, hast gained any Light, either from the Interpretation of Basilius, or my Commentaries, enjoy it, and communicate the same to the Sons of Art, that Philosophy oppressed for so many Years with the intollerable Yoak of Avarice, may at length be revived, and a return be of those times of Egyptians, in which Trismegistus and so many wise Magi, Philosophized not with empty denominations, but with wonderful Works.

In these, I think I have done my part, and writ more then sufficiently of Antimony. If any One follows me, he may add his own Experiences to these, that (with the singular favour of GOD) before the consummation of the World, the Mysteries of the most High may be revealed, to his Glory and honour, and the Conservation of health. Having finished this Discourse, I intend for a time to be silent and return to my Monastery, there to learn Philosophy further, that I may be able to comment of other Thigns and as I have already promised, I shall (GOD willing) write of Vitriol, common Sulphur, and the Loadstone, and open their Principle, Powers, Operations, and Virtues.

Let GOD the Lord of Heaven and Earth grant to us temporal Health here, and hereafter Eternal Salvation for the Refreshment of our Souls, in the Seas of Joy and Gladness, never to be limited within any Bounds of time. Amen.

Thus I conclude this Treatise of Antimony, and all whatsoever I have written of the Red Oil of Antimony, which is made of its Sulphur highly purified, and of the Spirit, which is prepared of its Salt. Incline your Mind to those, and with them compare these last, which I have prescribed you touching the Stone of Fire. If you acutely consider them, you may easily find their Union unto the End, by this Comparation. For the Foundation is the same, the Reason the same, the Friendship the same, by which Health is required, and the Stag long sought taken with a pleasant Hunting.

FINIS.

Parchment Books is committed to publishing high quality
Esoteric/Occult classic texts at a reasonable price.

With the premium on space in modern dwellings, we also strive - within the limits of good book design - to make our products as slender as possible, allowing more books to be fitted into a given bookshelf area.

Parchment Books is an imprint of Aziloth Books, which has established itself as a publisher boasting a diverse list of powerful, quality titles, including novels of flair and originality, and factual publications on controversial issues that have not found a home in the rather staid and politically-correct atmosphere of many publishing houses.

Titles Include:

Psychic Self-Defence	Dion Fortune
The Ancient Wisdom	Annie Besant
The Masters and the Path	C W Leadbeater
Man, His True Nature & Ministry	Louis-Claude de St.-Martin
Secret Doctrines of the Rosicrucians	Magus Incognito
Corpus Hermeticum	(trans. GRS Mead)
The Virgin of the World	Hermes Trismegistus
Raja Yoga	Yogi Ramacharaka
Theosophy	Rudolf Steiner
The Interior Castle	St Teresa of Avila
The Gospel of Thomas	Anonymous
Pistis Sophia	(trans. GRS Mead)
The Signature of All Things	Jacob Boehme
The Secret Destiny of America	Manly P Hall
Practical Mysticism	Evelyn Underhill
The Rosicrucian Mysteries	Max Heindel
The Conference of Birds	Farid ud-Din Attar
Meetings With Remarkable Men	G I Gurdjieff
The Everlasting Man	G K Chesterton
The Voice of the Silence	H P Blavatsky
War Is A Racket	Maj.-General Smedley D. Butler

Obtainable at all good online and local bookstores.

View Parchment Books' full list at: www.azilothbooks.com

We are a small, approachable company and would love to hear any of your comments and suggestions on our plans, products, or indeed on absolutely anything.   Aziloth is also interested in hearing from aspiring authors whom we might publish. We look forward to meeting you. Contact us at:

info@azilothbooks.com.

CATHEDRAL CLASSICS

Parchment Book's sister imprint, Cathedral Classics, hosts an array of classic literature, from ancient tomes to twentieth-century masterpieces, all of which deserve a place in your home. A small selection is detailed below:

Mary Shelley	*Frankenstein*
H G Wells	*The Time Machine; The Invisible Man*
Niccolo Machiavelli	*The Prince*
Omar Khayyam	*The Rubaiyat of Omar Khayyam*
Joseph Conrad	*Heart of Darkness; The Secret Agent*
Jane Austen	*Persuasion; Northanger Abbey*
Oscar Wilde	*The Picture of Dorian Gray*
Voltaire	*Candide*
Bulwer Lytton	*The Coming Race*
Arthur Conan Doyle	*The Adventures of Sherlock Holmes*
John Buchan	*The Thirty-Nine Steps*
Friedrich Nietzsche	*Beyond Good and Evil*
George Eliot	*Silas Marner*
Henry James	*Washington Square*
Stephen Crane	*The Red Badge of Courage*
Ralph Waldo Emmerson	*Self-Reliance, and Other Essays, (series 1&2)*
Sun Tzu	*The Art of War*
Charles Dickens	*A Christmas Carol*
Fyodor Dostoyevsky	*The Gambler; The Double*
Virginia Wolf	*To the Lighthouse; Mrs Dalloway.*
Johann W Goethe	*The Sorrows of Young Werther*
Walt Whitman	*Leaves of Grass - 1855 edition*
Confucius	*Analects*
Anonymous	*Beowulf*
Anne Bronte	*Agnes Grey*
More	*Utopia*
Farid ud-Din Attar	*The Conference of Birds*
Jack London	*Call of the Wild*
Edwin A. Abbott	*Flatland*

full list at: www.azilothbooks.com

Obtainable at all good online and local bookstores.

Lightning Source UK Ltd.
Milton Keynes UK
UKHW020029261022
411081UK00009B/468